A PERSONAL TRUE STORY

How To Have Your Second Comforter

Anonymous

Hope is believing, faith is asking,
knowledge is receiving, and priesthood is becoming.

ISBN: 978-1-944200-17-6

Digital Legend Press Salt Lake City, UT

For copies, go to www.digitalegend.com or call 877-222-1960

"After a man so devotes himself to righteousness that his calling and election is made sure, then it will be his privilege to receive the other Comforter . . . Now what is this other Comforter? It is no more or less than the Lord Jesus Christ Himself; and this is the sum and the substance of the whole matter; that when any man obtains this last Comforter, he will have the personage of Jesus Christ to attend him, or appear unto him from time to time, and even He will manifest the Father unto him, and they will take up their abode with him, and the visions of the heavens will be opened unto him, and the Lord will teach him face to face, and he may have a perfect knowledge of God . . ." Joseph Smith (*HC* 3:381.)

Table of Contents

The views expressed in this book are from the author's own personal experience, and are not officially sanctioned by the Church of Jesus Christ of Latter-day Saints.

The author has declined to receive any profits from the sale of this book.

About the Cover

The cover of this book is fairly straightforward in its meaning and intent, but the statement at the bottom of the cover page may be confusing to some. This is a phrase that was given to me a few years ago, by revelation, and has proven to me to be a very accurate progression of how to come to the Lord.

Hope is believing, faith is asking,
knowledge is receiving, and priesthood is becoming.

To have hope is to believe the promise from the Lord that we can indeed come to Him,[1] see His face, and know for ourselves that He lives. This hope becomes an anchor to our soul[2] as we pursue our Second Comforter experience. We must believe in order to plant the seed and begin the process.

Once we plant the seed in our heart we must nourish the desire that we may obtain the prize.[3] This requires us to exercise faith, which we do by asking God for that which we desire.[4] The asking and reaching, and endeavoring to pierce the veil is required to come to Him.[5] This is where the Holy

---

[1] Moroni 7:41-43, Romans 8:24-25

[2] Hebrew 6:19

[3] Alma 32:37-43

[4] James 1:6, Matthew 21:22

[5] James 2:20

Spirit[6] teaches us all we need in order to become a Son or Daughter of God, and to be reborn in the Spirit, new in Jesus Christ.[7]

Through the spirit of revelation, we receive knowledge[8] of the virtues of God and the mysteries of godliness, and we are able to receive our baptism of fire and come into the Lord's presence.

Finally, as we become one with the Father, the Son, and the Holy Ghost, we join the Church of the Firstborn and eventually receive a fullness of the priesthood. In doing so, we become as the Gods, knowing all things, as we bring to pass all righteousness according to our Father's will.[9]

There is a lot in that short statement, and by this path we can walk with God in His fullness and glory, even the Second Comforter, Jesus Christ.

---

[6] 1 John 3:1-3

[7] Mosiah 5:7, Mosiah 27:25, Alma 5:14, John 3:3, Moses 6:59

[8] Ephesians 1:17, 1 Nephi 10:19

[9] D&C 84:33-38

Introduction

This is no imaginary tale. You can part the veil and stand in the presence of God while you are still among the living. You *can* have this special gift called the Second Comforter.

This experience is no less than to be an actual witness of Jesus Christ; to hold Him and touch the marks in His hands, feet, and side; to hear Him tell you who you are, and bless you. And then your education truly begins, as God unfolds to you the mysteries.

I did not want to write this book but I was instructed to because it would help others. I am a witness of Him, but for now, I am to limit what I share and how I share it. The day will come when I and many others will stand in public, and before the world, to make it known that the day of the Lord is come. But at this time, my effort is to assist those who need to awaken and come to know the Lord.

Awake and Arise

Chapter One

I am a man over forty years old, married, and have been a member of the LDS Church my entire life. You might say I'm your average Joe, except for my spiritual side. For most of my life I have had one foot in the real world, and the other trying to make sense of what I cannot see. If there was anything about me that perhaps gave me an edge in this unrelenting adventure it would be a constant curiosity for things spiritual.

My parents and siblings are very normal. We don't have any fat skeletons in our closet, more than any other average middle class family. I attended church (still do), did scouting, said prayers, and ate casserole dinners. Yep, pretty basic life; but there were a few life changing moments that may have set the stage.

When I was still a young boy I saw two close relatives pass away. It was a great amount of grief for a little boy. I found myself being very contemplative. I thought often about where my family was on the other side and what they were doing. What is God like? Does He love me? Why do people suffer? I asked a lot of questions to my parents and they would share what they learned out of inspirational books and scripture. I believed in God with all my heart and wondered about my future.

I wasn't yet 12 years old when I had a profound spiritual experience. I desired to know if Joseph Smith was a prophet and I knelt down and asked God if it were true. I still remember the powerful feeling that washed over me. It was tangible and real and made me cry for a long time, which a tough boy like myself found a little unnerving. There was an audible voice in my head that responded to my question. I took this as my first brush with something beyond the veil.

My teen years were pretty basic. I wasn't a bad kid, but no saint either. I made a few mistakes, but chose to serve a mission at nineteen. I went to the temple and got my endowment. The temple seemed so mysterious to me and I wondered more about the things of God. What is He like? Can I really see Him in this life?

The mission lasted two long years. I worked hard, prayed hard, and studied hard. I tried to make sense of everything that was happening to me. There was much I didn't understand, and this became all the more apparent to me as I taught the Gospel and did missionary work in the field. I talked with other Elders about their thoughts regarding "Calling and Election and Second Comforter." Most of them felt that was something which occurred in the next life unless we are lucky enough to see the Second Coming.

I wondered about the Spirit and how it communicated to me. Was I having spiritual experiences? Was the Spirit with me when my heart was filled with love for the people, or when the scriptures really resonated in my mind? Was this the Spirit?

Even though I had taught the Moroni 10:4 scripture (which teaches us how to know the truth of all things) many times on my mission, I still wondered if I understood what God was trying to tell me.

Coming home from my mission brought mixed feelings. It was a happy reunion, but I felt anxiety for the future. I asked, now what? Where do I go from here spiritually?

Do you see how ordinary I am at this point? I want you to understand this so that you will not think I had some great advantage from my circumstances. I have often thought about those who have had powerful visionary or angelic experiences and wondered, "How could I hope for such things? Why are they special? Does the Lord love them more, or is their spirit just stronger than mine?" I would consider my situation and feel inferior and plain, like I was a nobody. Why would God visit me? (I will tell you that the Lord seeks out the "nobody's." It is through the small and simple that the Lord manifests Himself.[10])

Life continued on, and I went to college and learned a little about the world. I became abundantly aware that God is not welcome in most places. School was a frustrating experience, but a necessary one for me to learn about how to deal with Babylon.

I had an epiphany one day as I read the famous scripture: "If any of you lack wisdom, let him ask of God, that giveth to all men liberally, and upbraideth not; and it shall be given

---

[10] Alma 37:6-7

him."[11] It occurred to me that this applied to not only which church is true, but everything in life! In an interesting way, I felt that since school had done little to teach me anything valuable, why can't I ask God to be my teacher? This new understanding began a process of going to the Lord in prayer and asking for help to learn from Him. It wasn't long before I began to see a bread crumb trail leading me along in my studies and decisions but I didn't know where exactly it was leading me.

Before long I found my lovely wife. Or you could say she found me. Marrying the right person is truly a blessing. I know this is true, because I have seen so many who have struggled in their marriages. It is hard to know for sure who you are marrying until you've been together for a while; but I loved my wife from the moment I saw her and her support has made a difference in my confidence to seek the Lord. I know people who have had deep marital problems and still were blessed to have their Second Comforter experience. Perhaps for them, it was a catalyst for this to happen. If you can bring your spouse along with you on this ride, you will be happy indeed. At least for me, the biggest bread crumb the Lord ever gave me was the girl of my dreams.

After we had been married about a year I had another spiritual experience that was a slap in the face. I had started to drift in my desires to know the Lord and keep his commandments. It wasn't anything major, by the world's standards. I was going to church less, watching movies that

---

[11] James 1:5

were perhaps a little too violent. My thoughts were on the "Great and Spacious Building."

One afternoon, as I sat reading, I felt a presence enter the room that began to scold me forcefully. I could hear words in my head saying, "YOU are responsible for your family. What are you doing? Repent, and get your life in order before it is too late!" I was uncomfortably shaken by the rebuke. It was very real to me, and I knew that somebody wanted to get my attention. I could not see him, but there was something very real about the experience. I told my wife what happened and we covenanted with the Lord to make Him first. I have wondered who it was who came to me that day.

I learned an interesting lesson in those early years. Nothing ever comes at a convenient time. It was never the best time to get married, but I did it anyway. It wasn't good timing to have our first child, but we did it anyway. We always had faith and trusted in the Lord, and the Lord opened up a path each time we exercised faith. We worked hard, kept the commandments, paid our tithing, did our home teaching and visiting teaching, magnified our callings, went to the temple regularly; so far so good. Then something started to happen. This is about 20 years ago.

I began to awake and arise.

FAITH LIKE THE BROTHER OF JARED

I've always had a deep love for the Book of Mormon. I've read it many times and studied it. I actually dissected it like I was trying to discover a hidden treasure.

I remember thinking to myself, "What makes the Book of Mormon so special? How is it different from other scripture?" I understood that it came directly to us through revelation; that it was from a pure source. The book demonstrated a pattern of pride and repentance among those ancient people, and it had more specific detail regarding the atonement and commandments. I wondered, although this was great, was there something I was missing?

In 1986, President Benson had given a famous talk telling the saints that we were still under condemnation for not taking seriously the New Covenant of the Book of Mormon.[12] What exactly is that? What were we not taking seriously? I don't remember ever hearing the Church formally declare that the Lord had lifted this condemnation.

I went back and saw that the condemnation was made in 1832, roughly two years after the Church was organized. What had the membership of the Church failed to do?

And your minds in times past have been darkened

---

[12] The Book of Mormon–Keystone of our Religion, President Ezra Taft Benson, Oct. 1986

> because of **unbelief**, and because you have **treated lightly the things you have received**—Which **vanity and unbelief** have brought the whole church under condemnation. And this condemnation resteth upon the children of Zion, even all. And they shall remain under this condemnation until they repent and remember the new covenant, even the Book of Mormon and the former commandments which I have given them, not only to say, but to do according to that which I have written—That they may **bring forth fruit meet for their Father's kingdom**; otherwise there remaineth a scourge and judgment to be poured out upon the children of Zion. (D&C 84:54-58)

Twice the Lord says that the children of Zion are under condemnation for "unbelief." Unbelief in what? It seems the "New Covenant" that brings forth "fruit" for the Father's kingdom was being neglected. The Lord was not happy with the Saints after only two years of the Church being organized; this condemnation has never been lifted. This condemnation was the almost complete failure of the saints to seek Him; in other words, to come to Him, to receive their Second Comforter, to taste of the fruit of the Tree of Life. It seems we need to learn more about this "fruit."[13]

---

[13] There are different views as to the interpretation of this scripture and the Lord's condemnation. Some suggest that the early saints had not done enough to spread the

One of the first stories told in the Book of Mormon is Lehi's Dream.[14] We read about his family trying to come to a tree to partake of a beautiful white fruit. It is a unique and deliberate teaching moment in the Book of Mormon. The fruit, we are told, is the "love of God,"[15] which we receive through Jesus Christ.

I read the chapters from the book of Jacob, where he tells the allegory of the Vineyard. There is a lot of talk about the "fruit" that the Lord is trying to bring forth and all the trouble He takes to make it happen.[16] What fruit do you think He's talking about?
Alma later gives his famous parable of the seed that is planted and grows into a tree that bears fruit.

> But if ye will nourish the word, yea, nourish the tree as it beginneth to grow, by your faith with great diligence, and with patience, looking forward

---

Gospel, particularly to the Native Americans (Lamanites). Today it is generally assumed that they were not reading the Book of Mormon with enough zeal. But if you closely examine the previous verses of Section 84 it speaks directly to the point that the Israelites had hardened their hearts and would not behold His face (D&C 84:23-24). Then the Lord explains the priesthood in detail, and the importance of doing all that He commands to receive a fullness.

[14] 1 Nephi 8

[15] 1 Nephi 11:22

[16] Jacob 5:72-77

> to the fruit thereof, it shall take root; and behold it shall be a tree springing up unto everlasting life. And because of your diligence and your faith and your patience with the word in nourishing it, that it may take root in you, behold, by and by ye shall pluck the fruit thereof, which is most precious, which is sweet above all that is sweet, and which is white above all that is white, yea, and pure above all that is pure; and ye shall feast upon this fruit even until ye are filled, that ye hunger not, neither shall ye thirst. Then, my brethren, ye shall reap the rewards of your faith, and your diligence, and patience, and long-suffering, waiting for the tree to bring forth fruit unto you. (Alma 32:41-43)

What is this fruit again? It is the love of God, manifest in His Son, as we come to Him and obtain the Second Comforter.

Toward the end of the Book of Mormon we learn of the Brother of Jared and his amazing encounter, where he is able to rend the veil and see the Lord.[17] Immediately after, Moroni explains the reason why the Brother of Jared was privileged to have this experience.

> And because of the knowledge of this man he could not be kept from beholding within the veil; and he saw the finger of Jesus, which, when he saw, he fell with fear; for he knew that it was the finger of the Lord; and he had faith no longer, for

---

[17] Ether 3:4-16

> he knew, nothing doubting. Wherefore, having this perfect knowledge of God, he could not be kept from within the veil; therefore he saw Jesus; and he did minister unto him. (Ether 3:19,20)

The Brother of Jared then has a vision where he is shown many things including all the inhabitants of the earth. He has his Second Comforter experience. Moroni then adds this:

> For he had said unto him in times before, that if he would believe in him that he could show unto him all things—it should be shown unto him; therefore the Lord could not withhold anything from him, for he knew that the Lord could show him all things. (Ether 3:26)

Moroni goes on to explain that the Brother of Jared saw many things of which were sealed, not to be given until the gentiles repent in the last days.[18] But then Moroni writes:

> And in that day that they shall exercise faith in me, saith the Lord, even as the brother of Jared did, that they may become sanctified in me, then will I manifest unto them the things which the brother of Jared saw, even to the unfolding unto them all my revelations, saith Jesus Christ, the Son of God, the Father of the heavens and of the earth, and all things that in them are. (Ether 4:7)

---

[18] Ether 4:6

That is a powerful promise. Do you think he's talking about you and me? Moroni goes on to share examples of others who have seen Christ[19] and he challenges the reader to do the same.

> And now, I would commend you to seek this Jesus of whom the prophets and apostles have written, that the grace of God the Father, and also the Lord Jesus Christ, and the Holy Ghost, which beareth record of them, may be and abide in you forever. Amen. (Ether 12:41)

I pondered this in my heart and wondered what were the chances that "little me" could experience the same thing?

Did the early members of the Church have much success in parting the veil? There were very few who received such things.[20] Did they establish Zion? Did they build the New Jerusalem and dwell with God like the City of Enoch? Apparently not. Why is that the case? If they couldn't, what chance do we have?

These kinds of thoughts kicked around in my head for a long time.

---

[19] Ether 12:19

[20] Joseph Smith, Oliver Cowdery, Lyman Wight, Levi Hancock, and other high priests who received Section 88 as they began the School of the Prophets were given the promise of Eternal Life, i.e. the Comforter. (D&C 88:4)

I thought more about Joseph Smith and his famous resolve after reading James 1:5 to ask God directly. We all know what that led to. I remembered for myself when I was younger asking God if Joseph was a prophet and receiving a powerful spiritual experience for making the effort.

I considered what the Brother of Jared did. He exercised great faith and somehow got the Lord's attention. Perhaps I could do something like that, really stick my neck out and do something awesome that would raise some eyebrows up there in heaven.

Each of us must have the courage and resolve to call down the blessings of heaven. The Brother of Jared gathered the 16 stones and asked the Lord to touch them;[21] Nephi was brave in acquiring the brass plates;[22] Enos prayed all night to have a remission of his sins;[23] Ammon went to the wicked Lamanites and risked his life to teach them the Gospel;[24] David faced Goliath;[25] and Joseph Smith went in to the grove seeking answers. [26]

I've thought about stories of people trying to get the attention of a prospective employer and going to great lengths to get the job. Often it's the person with the most

---

[21] Ether 3:1-5

[22] 1 Nephi 3:7

[23] Enos 1:4

[24] Alma 17:20-21

[25] 1 Samuel 17

[26] Joseph Smith—History 1:14

resilience, creativity, and perseverance that wins the prize. What could I do that would get the attention of the Lord?

> Let us here observe that after any members of the human family are made acquainted with the important fact that there is a God who has created and does uphold all things, the extent of their knowledge respecting his character and glory will depend upon their diligence and faithfulness in seeking after him, until, like Enoch, the brother of Jared, and Moses, they shall obtain faith in God and power with him to behold him face to face. (Lectures on Faith 2:55)

We are not just invited to experience what they did, but are expected and even commanded to do this. I had so much unbelief that I needed to shed in order to begin this journey. The belief, or "tradition," that these things are only for the ancient prophets is utterly false. Don't believe it! Consider the literal words of scripture:

> For he that diligently seeketh shall find; and the mysteries of God shall be unfolded unto them, by the power of the Holy Ghost, as well in these times as in times of old, and as well in times of old as in times to come; wherefore, the course of the Lord is one eternal round. (1 Nephi 10:19)

One summer morning I decided to give it a try; to be creative, resilient, courageous, and do something a little crazy. I drove a couple of hours and went far out in the desert to a place where I had planned to seek the Lord. I walked up a mountain and found a spot I was reasonably sure was private and undefiled by any previous visitors; it was my place. I made an altar from a pile of rocks and said a prayer to the Lord expressing my desires. I asked: "Lord, help me to have *faith like the brother of Jared*."

I fell asleep by the rocks and when I awoke a couple hours later I had the impression the Lord was smiling down on me. (Not to mention, a bad sunburn.) Nothing miraculous happened. I just listened to the sound of the wind blowing and wondered if I had wasted my time coming there that day.

The reason I share this experience is not to impress upon you that I did something unique and earth shattering. I've since heard that many God seekers have done similar things in their quest to find the Lord. This was the starting point of my story. I just asked. I wanted to experience or see something like the Brother of Jared. Is it wrong to hope for something like that? Am I presumptuous to think that God would speak with me? This was my first time doing something outside of the box of spiritual conventionality. This happened up in the mountains about 20 years ago. It's taken me that long to come to where I am today. That doesn't mean it will take you the same amount of time. In fact, I'm convinced that if you do it right, you will undoubtedly receive the Lord much sooner than I. I'm not exaggerating when I say that, or giving you false hope. The times in which we live are speeding up and I do believe the call to "awake and arise" is NOW.[27]

Believe me when I say you can do this, and it all begins with asking the question: "Lord, wilt thou help me to have faith like the brother of Jared? Help me to come unto thee."

---

[27] Moroni 10:31-33

The Struggle
Chapter Two

When an individual starts down the path of becoming familiar with the Lord, they should beware and proceed with caution. I didn't know what I was getting myself into when I first went up to the mountain. Wouldn't it be nice if it was as simple as taking an order from a drive thru window? For me, it was more like signing up to run a marathon. Consider these three requests and how the Lord might respond:

1. Help me to learn humility.
2. Help me to learn how to be patient.
3. Help me to have faith like the Brother of Jared

I'm saying we need to be careful what we ask the Lord, because He just might give it you. The part we often fail to consider is that there is a price to be paid for the gift.

> There is a law, irrevocably decreed in heaven before the foundations of this world, upon which all blessings are predicated—And when we obtain any blessing from God, it is by obedience to that law upon which it is predicated. (D&C 130:20, 21)

The price we are required to pay is called obedience. The Lord will ask you to do certain things—unordinary things, peculiar things, unconventional tasks—that will surely try your faith. You may be required to follow a trail of bread crumbs, not knowing beforehand the things which you should do.[28] In so doing, you will come to know the Lord. Your test may require you to step into the dark. It may ask you to endure terrible hardship, but you will learn to trust the Lord in the process.

Consider Lehi's family. When Lehi prayed to the Lord regarding Jerusalem, the Lord showed him what would happen if the Israelites did not repent.[29] Lehi was commanded to take his family and go into the wilderness. He didn't know where he was going, but he did know that he would be led to a land of promise.[30] I'm sure he never expected the kind of struggles and suffering his family would endure.

How could the Lord be this way? Why did they have to eat raw meat, go without food, their women give birth under such duress? Did they not murmur in their tribulations?[31] What lessons do we, as the reader, gain from Nephi's written account of it?

Not long after I prayed for "Jared faith," I began to enter my own wilderness experience.

---

[28] 1 Nephi 4:6
[29] 1 Nephi 1:18
[30] 1 Nephi 2:20
[31] 1 Nephi 16:19-20

Things became very difficult financially, as I struggled with a change in careers. I had to have help from the Bishop for two months and that was hard for me. Men are proud, and when it comes to being the provider, nothing was more humiliating than needing to ask for help. For two months, until I could get on my feet, I would work at the Bishop's Storehouse to justify the "free stuff" I was given. I felt abandoned by the Lord and deeply depressed, but priesthood blessings would remind me that the Lord was with me and my family. The Lord promised we would always have what we needed.

This was a time of great testing for me. My children were struggling with physical ailments, my career was dead, and we had little of anything. My wife was so supportive and kind and full of encouragement, but at times I could see the pain in her eyes. Why was my life falling apart?

I found myself at times murmuring to the Lord, "Why me? Why aren't you helping me?" After repenting and submitting to the Lord, I found myself numb to the hardships. I found a little job and resolved to make the best of things and just trust in the Lord.

I was just starting to feel happy in my humble circumstances when the flood gates opened and a bigger portion of the Lord's blessings began to pour in. My career took a miraculous turn, which opened the means for me to come to the "promised land," so to speak. I had passed one test; now I would need to learn another lesson.

DO YOU LOVE ME MORE THAN THESE?

Almost overnight my career changed. It was exciting and satisfying to see my business explode, as my products sold and recognition followed. Everything was happening so fast. I began to experience financial independence, a new house, and more freedom than before.

In retrospect, perhaps because of my previous "wilderness experience," I remembered the Lord and decided not to let the success overcome me. We chose to live within our means, not to have excesses. Our home was modest and I never took my success or fortune as a sign of my accomplishment but as a direct blessing of the Lord. We were generous to others in our money and time, and I chose to make unconventional business decisions, based on the Lord's direction, because I felt it would please Him.

There were many crossroads where I could hear the Lord ask me, "Lovest thou me more than these?"[32] And I would see myself having to make choices that seemed suicidal, from a business standpoint, only to see God's hand and mercy upon me and my family.

During all of these worldly blessings I felt a need to show the Lord that He had my heart. My focus turned to doing things that were defined by service. Although I wasn't consciously thinking that I could earn points with the Lord, I seemed to feel a need to be perfect in many ways.

---

[32] John 21:15

I became the mighty home teacher. I actually had some great experiences with various families over the years; we developed great and eternal friendships. I even saw an entire family sealed in the temple. This gave me great joy, and I would wonder if perhaps the Lord would open up His doors to me a little more because of my efforts.

I served in many capacities in the ward and in leadership roles. I wondered whether my status in leadership was a measure of my worthiness to the Lord. Did he rate me like this? Was the Stake President closer to the Lord than the Bishop? Was an area authority less in tune than say an Apostle? Does President Monson have daily chats with Jesus Christ in his office? Do you think he really sees him?

Why don't we ever hear about the Church leaders having Joseph Smith experiences? These questions would turn my thoughts back to Sunday School lessons where we were told that such things are too sacred to share, and that all that is required for us is to have faith and endure to the end; meaning, have a temple recommend and follow your priesthood leaders.

Those last two paragraphs may seem facetious, but they are not. This is not a book about the Church. I love the Church, for it is the means by which I received the Book of Mormon and much that has blessed my life. What I have learned is that the Lord wants us to come to Him, not the Church.

Many latter-day saints have placed the Church between them and the Lord. How is that? I have heard many members say things like, "I won't worry about it until the prophet says something about it." There are members that truly believe that if they have a temple recommend they have reached their pinnacle of salvation in this life.

The Lord began to open my understanding as if to say, "You must come to me, and only me. I am the way, the truth and the light. I stand at the gate and will let you enter, if that is your desire."

THE ARM OF FLESH

About this time in my life the Lord taught me some valuable lessons. I really seemed to put a lot of trust in people who I felt were God's messengers to me. I would take careful note of what the Bishop would say, or my Stake President. I didn't really trust myself enough, because, "What if I was deceived? These brethren can't screw up, but I sure can." We all know that every calling is from the Lord and that if we do what our priesthood leaders tell us we can never go astray. Isn't that right?

What about priesthood blessings? How often were these from the Lord, or just good folks with good intentions? Was my faith lacking for asking these questions?
One such brother who I highly respected prophesied to me on many occasions and I was crushed when I realized, after much faith in his words, that they were false. Why did I feel good in my heart when I prayed about what he had said? How am I to understand personal revelation if I don't know

whether it is from the Lord or myself? Who do I trust? Nephi gave a direct answer:

> O Lord, I have trusted in thee, and I will trust in thee forever. I will not put my trust in the arm of flesh; for I know that cursed is he that putteth his trust in the arm of flesh. Yea, cursed is he that putteth his trust in man or maketh flesh his arm. (2 Nephi 4:34)

Nephi uses the word "cursed" to describe those who put their trust in man. The most dreadful curse God can decree upon us is to be shut out from His presence.[33]

"It is better to trust in the LORD than to put confidence in man." (Psalms 118:8) This scripture teaches a most profound truth. Is this not the crux that prevents many from coming to the Lord? When the Lord asks, "Do you love me more than these?" is he referring to possessions? Could He also be referring to where we place our trust? In whom we place our trust? If we place any person between us and the Lord are we not guilty of idolatry?

These were many of the questions that I considered as I sought my Second Comforter. I decided that if I was going to find the Lord, it would be by going directly to Him, and not by means of any other person.

---

[33] Jeremiah 17:5, 1 Nephi 2:21, Alma 36:30

Learn of Me

Chapter Three

At the end of 2013 I heard the Lord's Spirit telling me I needed to volunteer to work at the temple. Shortly thereafter, I began working during the week as a volunteer ordinance worker. For one year I did this with great zeal and attention. It gave me much time to think and ponder the meaning behind the mysteries of the temple.

I had many questions. I wondered why there had been significant changes to the ordinances, both the Washing and Anointing and the Endowment. I wondered why the new films were so theatrical and had become more so with each new film release. Sometimes I would feel a beautiful spirit and at other times, for reasons I couldn't understand, I would sense darkness around me.

I would often imagine what it would be like to actually cross the veil and see Heavenly Father. Would I need to give all those signs and tokens to the angels or to the Lord Himself? How many of the people that I see attending the temple have had their Calling and Election Made Sure? How many have stood in the presence of the Lord? Have any of them?

I actually had a couple of profound spiritual experiences in the temple, where I saw through the veil and witnessed angels. Both times I had to really think, "Did I just see what I think I saw?" Although the encounters were vivid, they were with my spiritual eyes. I know this book would be more exciting if I shared what these were, but again, the purpose of the book is for you to learn how you can have your own Second Comforter experience.

After I had worked in the temple for a year, the Spirit in a very firm way told me, "It is enough, you need to now resign your position as an ordinance worker." I wasn't sure why, but followed the impression. This was the end of 2014.

WELCOME TO THE WORLD WIDE WEB

What an amazing time to live in the history of the world. There is so much knowledge at our fingertips. With information moving and expanding at such a high speed, many people become lost in all the conflicting viewpoints. For a seeker of truth there is much to sift through.

I reflected on my studies over the years. I have always had an interest in the topic of the Second Comforter and coming to the Lord and have researched all I could find about it.

I read all the works of Bruce R. McConkie, because he seemed to touch a little on the subject. Of course I poured over the writings of Joseph Smith, and the Doctrine of Covenants. Hugh Nibley talked about the deep stuff regularly; I got all his books. Overall, there is a pretty big hole or void on the subject of seeing the Lord in the flesh, and the church was relatively quiet on the topic.

My close friends and I used to swap stories of older members who told tales of knowing people who had received mysterious calls from the office of the First Presidency: to meet the prophet in the temple at a special time, be taken to the Holy of Holies, and receive their Calling and Election and Second Anointing. They were usually mission presidents, general authorities, close to the Brethren. Was that my only chance of getting close to the Lord in this life? Did the Lord only come to these lucky souls when they entered the Holy of Holies of the temple?

In recent years there have been some books that suggested it is worthy and proper for one to seek such a thing, such as John Pontius' book, "Following the Light of Christ into His Presence," and Denver Snuffer's book, "The Second Comforter." Many other books are now available, and there are more people starting to come forward claiming to have received a Second Comforter Experience.

I began to study these people's accounts and wondered, "Is it true?" For some I have to admit I was suspicious, or doubtful. Perhaps they conjured up something and were seeking attention, or just thought they saw something, but were either confused or delusional. I had learned the lesson not to trust in the arm of flesh; I wasn't going to get tricked.

Should someone who claimed to have his Second Comforter experience be dismissed as a tool of the devil if he used swear words or was excommunicated for the putting the church in a bad light? When I prayed, thinking I knew the answer, the Lord very patiently showed me that things are not always as they seem. Again, I was told to "relax." The Spirit was teaching me something.

I went through several months of reading blogs and Facebook Group pages. There was lots of different chatter. I found that some factions were very angry at the church. People were discussing topics of gay marriage, women and the priesthood, polygamy, racism, apostasy, and every imaginable subject of derision. I felt inclined to become familiar with the topics, but I didn't see the need to become a part of the negative discourse. I didn't feel anger or judgment towards the Church. I just wanted to know what the Lord wanted me to do.

I found myself sharing what I had learned about receiving revelation and dealing with the Adversary. This seemed to raise a few eyebrows even though I kept the information minimal. Some I shared with were very interested and thoughtful, and some became agitated and incredulous. "Prove it in the scriptures!" was the answer of choice. By all accounts that is a good remedy, but for some things it requires us to go to the Lord so that we can receive our own personal revelation in order to learn the truth for ourselves.

> Draw near unto me and I will draw near unto you; seek me diligently and ye shall find me; ask, and ye shall receive; knock, and it shall be opened unto you. (D&C 88:63)

After three months of engaging in these forums I quietly disconnected from the internet groups and asked the Lord, "Now what?"

From here I began a part of my journey where I saw the Lord teaching me and guiding my studies. I was particularly focused on understanding the process of revelation. I learned about the Gifts of the Spirit and prayer and sought to understand more of the mysteries of godliness. Some of these concepts that I believe had an impact for me have been included in this book. The chapters on the Adversary, revelation, prayer, visions, and angels were written during this time. Some of them have been modified, as my understanding recently after my experience with the Lord has clarified some principles.

Receiving Revelation

Chapter Four

My journey took a sharp turn toward the Lord when I began to learn about receiving revelation. I have put these principles together in a way that you can understand as quickly as possible. Applying these principles will take practice and effort, but, like learning to play an instrument or speak a foreign language, you too will be able to learn them and find what you are seeking.

How do we receive pure revelation and know it's the real thing? Are we not seeking knowledge that will lead us to Christ, literally? I would like to share some ideas that have made a huge difference for me. This pattern involves prayer, asking questions, and developing sensitivity to hearing the voice of the Lord and His messengers.

Where do you start?

OBSTACLES

It's so important to know that the Lord is guiding us and that we're on the right path. Receiving revelation can be troublesome when distracted by the challenges of life, if bad spirits are controlling us because of sin and addiction, or if our emotions have enough power over us to cloud our thoughts. The Adversary uses many devices to prevent us from succeeding: fear and discouragement are two of his favorites. If our preconceived ideas of how the Lord will communicate with us overshadow our desire to ask the Lord in faith, we will struggle to get answers. [34] First, we must clear our thoughts, relax, and focus. Then, when we are in that quiet mode of pondering, the Lord can easily speak to us through His Spirit.

WHAT IS IT?

Beginning the process of learning to receive revelation may be confusing. We ask questions and wait to hear something, but what are we expecting to hear? Will it be an audible voice? Will it be a warm feeling? Many have been conditioned by years of Sunday School to expect a "burning in the bosom"[35] or some miraculous event. Some waiting to get that feeling simply give up until they start to cry in Sacrament Meeting because somebody shared a sentimental story; they wonder if they now have had a spiritual witness. Typically, revelation comes as a soft, mild voice in the mind or a clear knowledge that rests upon the soul "like the dews from Heaven."[36]

> When you feel pure intelligence flowing into you, it may give you sudden strokes of ideas, so that by noticing it, you may find it fulfilled the same day or soon; (i.e.) those things that were presented unto your minds by the Spirit of God, will come to pass;

[34] Jarom 1:4

[35] D&C 9:8

[36] D&C 121:45

> and thus by learning the Spirit of God and understanding it, you may grow into the principle of revelation, until you become perfect in Christ Jesus. (Teachings of the Prophet Joseph Smith, sel. Joseph Fielding Smith [1976], 151.)

START SMALL

For many of us we have to "grow into the principle of revelation." Some advice for learning to hear "The Voice" may be to start by asking closed-ended questions that can be answered with either a "yes" or "no" answer. If the answer is unclear, I would repeat the question a second or third time to see if you get the same answer. If there is a confused feeling, don't assume the answer is no. Consider rephrasing the question or ask a different question until a response comes. The answer should give you a settled, comfortable feeling.

An example of a conversation in prayer may be as follows:

"Lord, how should I spend my time?" (No answer.) "Lord, should I spend more time with my family?" (Yes.)

A question that is too broad may not be answered. We need to ask questions that the Lord can properly answer. Often the Spirit will lead us to know what to say and how to ask the actual question. As our understanding of the Spirit grows we can receive more than the single word response. Remember, one must get good at asking questions if they want to be good at getting answers. Ask LOTS of questions, humbly, patiently, and expect to get an answer to each question.[37] It requires concentration of the mind and heart both working together in harmony.

EVER TRIED THIS?

I would suggest having a pencil and paper to write the answers as they come to you. You can even write questions beforehand so they can be read to the Lord while praying. Closing your eyes and kneeling are not always necessary. Try sitting down on the ground to get comfortable. As answers come, write them down. Perhaps spend more time pondering than speaking the prayer. The Lord will often present visions in your mind as your focused thoughts ponder on the topic. [38]

As you progress into the principle of revelation, you will begin to receive more than just "yes and no" answers. Phrases will come to you, and phrases will grow into longer sentences, and sentences into conversations, as you find yourself speaking by the Power of the Holy Ghost to someone on the other side of the veil. [39]

LIKE A BLESSING

For those who have given a priesthood blessing, the act of receiving revelation is similar. We clear our minds and say

---

[37] James 1:5-6

[38] 1 Nephi 11:1

[39] 2 Nephi 28:30

what comes, removing any preconceptions and simply trusting the Lord. The spirit provides the intelligence and our brains translate the thoughts into words.

WILL I BE DECEIVED?

Some people may begin to feel nervous and ask, "What if I am deceived?" It is important to sometimes ask the Lord to shield us from the Adversary. It is easy to be deceived if we are too eager to gain knowledge and don't check our answers.[40] I often ask, "Lord, are there any spirits here that need to be removed?" If yes, I simply ask Him what to do and follow the instruction. [41]

If you are struggling with the ability to receive revelation, ask the Lord if He will give this gift to you.[42] Asking opens the doors of Heaven.[43] I call this the "Law of Asking."

Moroni gives his council to those seeking an understanding of truth verses error:

> Wherefore, a man being evil cannot do that which is good; neither will he give a good gift. For behold, a bitter fountain cannot bring forth good water; neither can a good fountain bring forth bitter water; wherefore, a man being a servant of the

---

[40] Mosiah 4:27

[41] D&C 46:7-8

[42] D&C 6:10-11

[43] 3 Nephi 27:29

> devil cannot follow Christ; and if he follow Christ he cannot be a servant of the devil. Wherefore, all things which are good cometh of God; and that which is evil cometh of the devil; for the devil is an enemy unto God, and fighteth against him continually, and inviteth and enticeth to sin, and to do that which is evil continually. But behold, that which is of God inviteth and enticeth to do good continually; wherefore, every thing which inviteth and enticeth to do good, and to love God, and to serve him, is inspired of God. Wherefore, take heed, my beloved brethren, that ye do not judge that which is evil to be of God, or that which is good and of God to be of the devil. (Moroni 7:10-14)

If you continue to ask and you cannot get a yes or no where just moments earlier it came easily—take it as a no.[44] Be sure you are asking with a clear mind, devoid of emotion, unworthy thoughts, or doubts that you are receiving revelation.[45] Remember, the Spirit will speak to you and you will often translate these messages into your own words; therefore the words will have a voice similar to your own and yet from above.[46] Do not be discouraged if you find that you were being deceived by the Adversary. You must be tempted that you may learn to distinguish the good from

---

[44] D&C 9:9

[45] Mormon 9:27-28

[46] D&C 8:2-3

the evil.[47] If you are humble and seek the Lord, you will be led to the truth.[48] There must be an opposition in all things;[49] therefore, if you are given a deception by the Adversary, prepare yourself to receive a powerful revelatory experience from the Lord, for He shall not leave you comfortless.[50]

We are all deceived during our lives and Satan is cunning. Many never find their way because they fail to exercise faith in the Lord and seek Him. For those who do seek Him, they are led to knowledge and freedom.

Fear of a deceptive witness can still prevent good people from even attempting to seek revelation or to part the veil. You must never fear such things.[51] The best avenue to knowing that your revelation is correct and from the Lord is to do the following:

1 Ask the Lord if there are any deceitful spirits near you. This is one question where the Lord has never allowed the Adversary to deceive me. You will know. Ask that a shield be placed around you to prevent your conversation from being heard or interrupted.
2 Ask if there is anything else you need to do in order to speak without deception with the Lord. The purpose

---

[47] Moses 6:55
[48] Moroni 10:4-5
[49] 2 Nephi 2:11
[50] John 14:18
[51] Isaiah 41:10

of this is to strengthen the shield if necessary. You can trust that the Adversary will not intercept your prayer.

3 Receive your revelation.

Check your revelation to see if it is accurate and inspired. Unless there is any part of the revelation that feels awkward or troublesome after this point,[52] embrace it as your personal scripture. If not, revisit that part in prayer. Never be afraid or doubt; be believing.

WHAT KINDS OF REVELATION?

The Lord may also reveal His will to us through dreams, visions, the scriptures, and the words of other people. Often the experience is more than a casual impression, more vivid than a fleeting thought, and makes a profound impact. But again, it is always good to check with the Lord. "Lord, is this revelation from thee? Is this truth?" And then we must forge ahead and believe.

WHAT NEXT?

After learning to receive revelation, the journey begins to expand exponentially. You are administered to by Angels and hear the voice of the Lord. You will be led to do all things the Lord would have you to do. This is a principle of faith that leads to the mysteries of godliness.[53] The Lord

---

[52] D&C 9:9

[53] 1 Nephi 10:19. You cannot receive revelation without exercising faith.

wants to bring us to Him as fast as we are willing to go.[54] It is difficult for many to trust that the Lord would speak to them directly, but He does. The journey of coming to know Him is rich in blessings as He thins the veil and you move toward the ultimate goal of knowing for yourself.

> Salvation cannot come without revelation; it is in vain for anyone to minister without it. No man is a minister of Jesus Christ without being a Prophet. No man can be a minister of Jesus Christ except he has [the] testimony of Jesus; and this is the spirit of prophecy. Whenever salvation has been administered, it has been by testimony. Men of the present time testify of heaven and hell, and have never seen either; and I will say that no man knows these things without this. (Joseph Smith, DHC v3. p.389)

I think there are many facets to this conversation worth exploring. We should never be afraid to ask questions and seek more understanding. Ask that the Lord to bestow His gifts upon you, specifically the Gift of Discernment. If we can't find our answer in the scriptures, and we've exhausted our resources, take it to the Lord and expect something from above. Expect the unexpected.

---

[54] 2 Nephi 28:30

Ten Stages of Revelatory Progression

Chapter Five

1 Feel the Spirit.
2 Hear a word in your mind.
3 Hear a phrase in your mind.
4 Have a conversation with the Lord.
5 Speak with messengers (angels, passed family, notable past spirits).
6 Learn to fight the Adversary (during all of the above).
7 See with your eyes numbers 5 and 6.
8 Experience the Savior.
9 Experience the Father.
10 Experience Heavenly Mother.

The Lord waits until the fourth watch to make His appearance.[55] If you want these experiences you need to ask, be patient, and follow the promptings no matter how odd they may seem. Be prepared, your life will never be the same.

---

[55] Matthew 14:25

Praying with Power

Chapter Six

We all understand the basic tenets of prayer, but what does it take to have a powerful prayer, the kind that shakes the Heavens and unlocks the keys to the "mysteries of godliness?" The Lord loves us so much that not even a hair of our head falls unnoticed;[56] He hears even the smallest prayer, but the way we pray can literally make all the difference. How is that? By learning how to ask, we learn how to effectively receive what He has to give us.

STEP ONE: AM I CLEAN?

I was taught this method from someone that was close to me. The words are not as important as the meaning behind them. Don't worry if parts of your prayer begin to sound repetitive. Focus on your feelings and even more on the responses you receive from the Spirit. I start by asking for forgiveness:

"Father, please forgive me for anything I may have done knowingly or unknowingly, which is contrary to thy will, thy laws, or commandments." I then listen and ponder on the thoughts that come to my mind. Sometimes I get a quick, "You are clean," or "You are forgiven," and move to the next step. Sometimes I realize I need to do a little repenting. (We

---

[56] Matthew 10:29-31, D&C 84:80

must be clean to unlock the door.)

STEP TWO: EXPRESS MY LOVE

I think of this step as reaching out to the Father by expressing my love and gratitude and praise for Him. "Lord, I love thee because . . ." I often see myself kneeling at the Throne of God and slowly moving toward Him. I wait until my heart is full of gratitude and I sense His love surround me. I spend as much time as it takes before I move to step three. (We've unlocked the door and approached Him.)[57]

STEP THREE: HELP ME

At this stage I humbly ask: "Lord, if it be thy will, wilt thou share thy love and light with me?" I then begin to ask His will regarding questions to which I need answers, blessings, or council. I actually see in my mind His light descending upon me. I'm careful to ask His will and not impose my stubborn desires into the conversation. (We have unlocked the door, approached Him, and felt His arms around us.)

STEP FOUR: HELP OTHERS

This may be the most important stage. As we seek to bless others we can literally extend that light toward those who need His blessings. This pleases God and helps us thin the veil even more. We should seek this with each prayer.

---

[57] I've since learned much more regarding this step, which I discuss in the section "Praise," pg. 134

"Father, if it be thy will, wilt thou share thy love and light with . . ." This stage usually requires the most effort as we seek out those in need and exercise creative faith in their behalf. (We have unlocked the door, approached Him, felt His arms around us, and shared with others.[58])

OUTWARD APPEARANCES

Most of us have been taught to pray by bowing our heads, closing our eyes, and clasping our hands.[59] This traditional approach comes from the Protestant traditions of the past. The Lord honors these prayers, but this is not how the Lord prayed, or the early Christian saints. My wife and I teach our children, when we pray, to kneel when possible and even sometimes to look up to God. At times it is appropriate to raise your arms as you express your love to Him. It is good to kneel whenever possible, but I often sit on the ground when I pray so that I can pray longer without my knees aching or my feet falling asleep. You can obviously pray anywhere: in the car, the shower, driving to work, at a party, everywhere. Why does it even matter what our body is doing when we pray? Only to the extent that it reflects our hearts. I like to use thee's and thou's when I pray because it feels more holy, and those words reflect my heart. For some it may be different. You can speak vocally or in your mind. For many, vocal prayers evoke stronger feelings of the heart. Sometimes I veil my prayers so the Adversary doesn't' know what I'm up to. Everything we do

---

[58] 3 Nephi 1:11, Ether 3:3, 1 Nephi 2:18, Mormon 3:12

[59] Matthew 6:5-15 (How to pray)

is a sign to God of our intentions.[60]

TAKE TIME TO BE HOLY

I would suggest taking time, at least once a day, to completely dedicate yourself to communicating with the Lord. I often do it in the middle of the night when everything is quiet in the house. Sometimes the morning is good. I like these times because I'm in a fasted state that makes it easier for me to focus on the Spirit. It's up to you when you do it, but it will make a huge difference in your prayers. In fact, as a seeker of greater gifts, you MUST take time to be holy. Holiness comes as we immerse ourselves in the Spirit and open ourselves to the Lord to receive communications from Him. (I will speak on this more in the coming chapters.)

A NOTE ABOUT FASTING

Someone could write an entire book on the subject, but it is important to make a note on the topic when discussing praying with power. Fasting can be any kind of sacrifice which involves the body. You can fast from food, water, sleep, dairy products, sugar and sweets, the internet, anything that your body craves. And instead of focusing on physical needs, focus on the purpose of your fast. These sacrifices clear the channels and revelation pours down more freely.

This method has worked miracles in my own life and my

---

[60] D&C 137:9

family. Once the initial prayer is given, continue praying throughout the day as step 2, 3, and 4 are offered in the heart and mind. The "principle of revelation" will begin to rest upon your soul as the "dews of Heaven,"[61] and your prayers will become filled with the spirit of revelation and the glory of God.

CRY UNTO THE LORD

Do you think that the emotion you generate when praying will make a difference? To cry usually means to communicate with great emotion and desire. I have found that in my quest to find my Second Comforter it was essential. Especially in receiving my Baptism of Fire and the Gift of the Holy Ghost. Having a broken heart and a contrite spirit[62] requires us to crawl to the Lord in a manner of speaking, and plead with Him to make us clean; then the door begins to open.

What does it mean to "cry unto the Lord?"

1 To pray with all your heart.[63]
2 To vocally express your prayer with great emotion.[64]
3 To feel it more than think it.
4 To let go of all pride.

---

[61] D&C 121:45

[62] Ether 4:15

[63] 2 Nephi 4:30, Mosiah 24:12, Alma 34:27, Mormon 9:27

[64] Psalms 77:1

5 To be like a child crying out for his parent to rescue them.
6 To become as a little child.
7 To cry for joy.
8 To cry for help.
9 To cry to be close to Him.
10 To cry to be fed and nourished.

There are many examples in scripture of crying unto the Lord. King David wrote the Book of Psalms, which by definition are a collection of written verses to praise God.

"The righteous cry, and the Lord heareth, and delivereth them out of all their troubles." (Psalms 34:17)

"When I cry unto thee, then shall mine enemies turn back: this I know; for God is for me." (Psalms 56:9)

"Evening, and morning, and at noon, will I pray, and **cry aloud**, and He shall hear my voice." (Psalms 55:17)

This is an interesting parable that sheds some light on this principle:

> And he spake a parable unto them to this end, that men ought always to pray, and not to faint; Saying, There was in a city a judge, which feared not God, neither regarded man: And there was a widow in that city; and she came unto him, saying, Avenge me of mine adversary. And he would not for a while: but afterward he said within himself,

Though I fear not God, nor regard man; Yet because this widow troubleth me, I will avenge her, lest by her continual coming she weary me. And the Lord said, Hear what the unjust judge saith. And shall not God avenge his own elect, which cry day and night unto him, though he bear long with them? I tell you that he will avenge them speedily. Nevertheless when the Son of man cometh, shall he find faith on the earth? (Luke 18:1-8)

When this man cried out the Lord healed him:

And they came to Jericho: and as he went out of Jericho with his disciples and a great number of people, blind Bartimaeus, the son of Timaeus, sat by the highway side begging. And when he heard that it was Jesus of Nazareth, he began to cry out, and say, Jesus, thou son of David, have mercy on me. And many charged him that he should hold his peace: but he cried the more a great deal, Thou son of David, have mercy on me.

And Jesus stood still, and commanded him to be called. And they call the blind man, saying unto him, Be of good comfort, rise; he calleth thee. And he, casting away his garment, rose, and came to Jesus. And Jesus answered and said unto him, What wilt thou that I should do unto thee? The blind man said unto him, Lord, that I might receive my sight. And Jesus said unto him, Go thy way; thy

> faith hath made thee whole. And immediately he received his sight, and followed Jesus in the way. (Mark 10:46-51)

The blind man had been crying out loud repeatedly, "Thou Son of David, have mercy on me." The cry had reached the ear of the Lord. Jesus knew what the man wanted and was ready to grant it to him. But before He did, He asked him, "What wilt thou that I should do unto thee?" He wanted to hear not only the general petition for mercy, but the distinct words of what the man's desire was that day. Until he verbalized it, he was not healed.

Then the crowd rebukes the noisy clamor of Bartimaeus. Despite the seeming unconcern of his Lord, however, and despite the rebuke of an impatient and quick-tempered crowd, the blind beggar still cries, and increases the loudness, until Jesus is impressed and moved.

"Then shalt thou call, and the LORD shall answer; thou shalt cry, and he shall say, Here I *am*." (Isaiah 58:9)

> And, behold, a woman of Canaan came out of the same coasts, and cried unto him, saying, have mercy on me, O Lord, thou son of David; my daughter is grievously vexed with a devil. But he answered her not a word. And his disciples came and besought him, saying, Send her away; for she crieth after us. But he answered and said, I am not sent but unto the lost sheep of the house of Israel. Then came she and worshipped him, saying, Lord,

> help me. But he answered and said, it is not meet to take the children's bread, and to cast it to dogs. And she said, Truth, Lord: yet the dogs eat of the crumbs which fall from their masters' table. Then Jesus answered and said unto her, O woman, great is thy faith: be it unto thee even as thou wilt. And her daughter was made whole from that very hour. (Matthew 15:22-28)

If this Canaanite woman's prayer had been without heart, it would have been empty. We must exert our full heart, might, mind, and soul when we pray.[65] Heaven must be made to feel the force of our prayers. As they say, "there must be a stirring below to have a stirring above."

> At first, Jesus appears to pay no attention to the Canaanite women's agony, and ignores her cry for relief. He gives her neither eye, nor ear, nor word. Silence, deep and chilling, greets her impassioned cry. But she is not turned aside, nor disheartened. She holds on. This last cry won her case; her daughter was healed in the self-same hour. Hopeful, urgent, and unwearied, she stays near the Master, insisting and praying until the answer is given. What a study in importunity, in earnestness, in persistence, promoted and

---

[65] Mark 12:30, D&C 59:5. Our "full heart" is our desire. Our "might or strength" is our energy of body. Our "mind" is our intellect. The "soul" is the essence of who we are that is closest to God.

> propelled under conditions which would have disheartened any but a heroic, a constant soul. [66]

"Prayer, without fervor, stakes nothing on the issue, because it has nothing to stake. It comes with empty hands. Hands, too, which are listless, as well as empty, which have never learned the lesson of clinging to the Cross. Fervor-less prayer has no heart in it; it is an empty thing, an unfit vessel. Heart, soul, and life, must find place in all real praying. Heaven must be made to feel the force of this crying unto God." (Robert Murray M'Cheyne, Church of Scotland, 1813-1843)

"The prayer that sparks revival begins long before the countryside seems to awaken from its slumber in sin. It starts when men fall on their knees and cry out to God. That's where true intimacy with God takes place and we begin the journey of being transformed into the image of Christ. And as men are transformed, the course of a nation can be changed." (Wellington Boone, Evangelical Christian, 1948-)

One thing about crying out is that only the desperate do this; are you desperate? God gives immediate attention to the people that cry out to Him. "And shall God not avenge His own elect who cry out day and night to Him, though He bears long with them? I tell you that He will avenge them

---

[66] The Complete Works of E. M. Bounds on Prayer, by E. M. Bounds

speedily." [67]

*"Go through the midst of the city, and set a mark upon the foreheads of the men that **sigh and cry** for all the abominations that be done in the midst thereof." (Ezekiel 9:4)*

> And it came to pass that I, Nephi, being exceedingly young, nevertheless being large in stature, and also having great desires to know of the mysteries of God, wherefore, **I did cry unto the Lord**; and behold he did visit me, and did soften my heart that I did believe all the words which had been spoken by my father; wherefore, I did not rebel against him like unto my brothers. (1 NE 2:16)

Nephi describes in detail, not just what he was praying for, but how he prayed; and the result was that the Lord visited him.

> And my soul hungered; and I kneeled down before my Maker, **and I cried unto him in mighty prayer** and supplication for mine own soul; and **all the day long did I cry unto him**; yea, and when the night came I did still raise my voice high that it reached the heavens. (Enos 1:4)

Imagine praying all day long with that kind of

---

[67] Luke 18:7-8

determination. Enos was visited by the Lord; how bad do you want it?

Alma gives us council for what to specifically cry for when we pray to the Lord:

> Yea, cry unto him **for mercy**; for he is mighty to save.
> Yea, humble yourselves, and continue in prayer unto him. Cry unto him when ye are in your fields, yea, over **all your flocks**. Cry unto him in your houses, yea, over **all your household**, both morning, mid-day, and evening. Yea, cry unto him **against the power of your enemies**. Yea, cry unto him **against the devil**, who is an enemy to all righteousness. Cry unto him **over the crops of your fields, that ye may prosper in them**. Cry over the **flocks of your fields, that they may increase.** Yea, and when you do not cry unto the Lord, let your hearts be full, drawn out in prayer unto him continually **for your welfare, and also for the welfare of those who are around you.** (Alma 34:18-27)

How does someone cry unto the Lord?

- Praise Him.
- Broken heart and contrite spirit.
- Plea for mercy.
- Speak vocally with emotion.
- Forget yourself, complete humility.

As members of the Church we have been taught to pray quietly and reverently. We have been trained to control our emotions, which is appropriate, but are there times when we should shout out in praise?[68] Could it be that when Moroni told the Daughters of Zion in the last chapter of the Book of Mormon to "awake and arise"[69] he meant to open ourselves in prayer and praise to the Lord both spiritually and literally and with great emotion?

Let us learn to cry unto the Lord with all our hearts. Let us allow our prayers to reach the heavens as never before.

LAW OF THE LAST SECOND

Have you ever had the experience of praying for guidance with all your heart, receiving an answer from the spirit, and then later finding out that it didn't work out as planned? Perhaps you prayed about a new job, a love interest, an important decision, but it just didn't happen as your revelation seemed to imply. You might even say it was a failure. What causes that? Did you make a mistake? Some of the greatest lessons we can learn are from our failures.

I was once given a blessing that was very specific and for years the promised blessings didn't occur. I would hold up

---

[68] The only instance where we do this in the church is the "Hallelujah Shout" upon the dedication of our temples.
[69] Moroni 10:31

a piece of paper with my notes from the blessing and cry out in my prayer, "Lord, on this day I received a blessing and this is what it said. When will thou help me?" As the years rolled on I didn't stop reminding the Lord, and when I was pretty much numb to it all, the blessing was manifested EXACTLY as it had been given.

I prayed once about investing my time in a business venture. I spent a lot of money and time and it was a flop. Why? I had prayed and received a confirmation. It turned out as I looked back on the experience that it set me up for a great blessing. The negative experience was a stepping stone to something wonderful. Sometimes you just have to trust the Lord. Remember, the Lord often works by the principle, "The Law of the Last Second."[70]

You're thinking, "What is that? Never heard of that before; show me in the scriptures!" There are many examples in the scriptures where prophets were tested: Lehi trying to get to the land of promise; Moses saved from the grasp of the Egyptians; Abraham almost sacrificing Isaac. The scriptures are full of these. But sometimes our plans and expectations just completely fail. This can occur because we don't live up

---

[70] Sometimes this is referred to as the Fourth Watch, referencing when Jesus came to the apostles on the Sea of Galilee during the storm. The Jews (as well as the Romans) usually divided the night into four watches of three hours each. The first watch began at six, the second at nine, the third at twelve, the fourth at three in the morning. (Matthew 14:25)

to our part of the bargain.

I wonder if the Lord has a flair for the dramatic ending, like an epic movie where the hero comes through at the last second. When it comes to the fulfillment of blessings and promises from the Lord, I have found the "last second rule" to be true so many times in my life that I have come to expect it. You need to exercise faith until the end, or should I say beyond that. When we try to set a date and convince ourselves that surely the Lord can't keep his promise beyond that day, we'll surely be disappointed. I find it best to not set a time frame and to just trust and wait patiently, for the Lord always keeps his promises.[71]

As I set out to have my Second Comforter experience I wondered if I would ever find what I was looking for. Was this an empty dream? Doubts and worries would occasionally cross my mind; and you know where those thoughts come from, don't you? You must believe, and hope, and ask, and endure. This is why I am writing this book; to give you hope. It has come true for me and it will happen to you as you follow His instructions.

---

[71] D&C 1:38

You Must Learn to Have Visions
Chapter Seven

Where does someone start to learn about the Gift of the Spirit that opens the door to visions? Must we wait for the Lord to help us? How is our "faith" involved in this process? Haven't we been promised that if we "knock" He shall open the door? These are the questions that I think are worth exploring.

WHAT IS A VISION?

Have you ever had a daydream where your mind drifts off into a fantasy and you see something that isn't really there? Sometimes we experience this as we read a book, listen to someone talk, or do a mundane task. We see in our mind what our eyes cannot. The difference between a daydream and a vision is that the Holy Spirit directs the "vision." It is holy, it has purpose, it is vivid, and the possibilities are glorious.

IS IT APPROPRIATE TO ASK FOR A VISION?

Nephi said, "For it came to pass after I had desired to know the things that my father had seen, and believing that the Lord was able to make them known unto me, as I sat pondering in mine heart I was caught away in the Spirit of the Lord, yea, into an exceedingly high mountain, which I never had before seen, and upon which I never had before set my foot." (1 Nephi 11:1) As Nephi sat pondering over his father's vision his own vision opened. He believed, he asked, and it was given to him.

"And there are many among us who have many revelations, for they are not all stiffnecked. And as many as are not stiffnecked and have faith, have communion with the Holy Spirit, which maketh manifest unto the children of men, according to their faith." (Jarom 1:4) The word, "stiffnecked" implies that they will not bend or look or do things they are unaccustomed to doing. Like a child who learns as they grow up that certain things are senseless (Santa, Easter Bunny, etc.), often the Gifts of the Spirit are placed in this category by the "older and wiser." If you can't touch it, feel it, or see it, don't believe it. Is it no coincidence that Christ said we are to become as a little child?

Perhaps it was Joseph's child-like faith that the Lord needed in his prophet. "It is my meditation all the day & more than my meat & drink to know how I shall make the saints of God to comprehend the visions that roll like an overflowing surge, before my mind."[72]

Can we open our minds to receive overflowing visions?

YES.

I believe that we are required to commune with the Spirit of God if we are to receive the ministering of angels and

---

[72] Writings of Joseph Smith, pg. 196

learn the mysteries of godliness. "Behold, I say unto you that whoso believeth in Christ, doubting nothing, whatsoever he shall ask the Father in the name of Christ it shall be granted him; and this promise is unto all, even unto the ends of the earth." [73]

WHY SHOULD YOU HAVE A VISION?

What is the purpose of having a vision? Ultimately, it is to educate and uplift you, to bring you closer to the Lord. Here are five good reasons one might experience a vision:

1. The Lord uses visions to impart **knowledge** to us in a dramatic fashion to instruct and to edify us. Most people are visual learners, and the impact of a vision is hard to forget.
2. We may see a vision of the future to provide **prophecy** of coming events.
3. A vision may come as a **warning** to motivate us to take action for our own safety and others.[74]
4. A vision may help you to **interpret dreams**, either for yourself or others.[75]
5. The purpose may be for you to be a **witness** of an important event or thing. The most important vision is where you become a witness of Jesus Christ.

Seeking a vision when our intent is pure is a righteous desire

---

[73] Mormon 9:21

[74] 2 Nephi 1:4, Lehi's vision of the destruction of Jerusalem

[75] Genesis 41, Daniel 4

and should be encouraged.

> Draw near unto me and I will draw near unto you; seek me diligently and ye shall find me; ask, and ye shall receive; knock, and it shall be opened unto you. Whatsoever ye ask the Father in my name it shall be given unto you, that is expedient for you; And if ye ask anything that is not expedient for you, it shall turn unto your condemnation. (D&C 88:63-65)

In what way could a vision not be expedient for you and displease the Lord? If the purpose of your seeking the vision is improper and not based on a righteous desire the Lord will not provide it. This is why it is good to check with the Lord before you begin. The Lord desires to bless you with these gifts—you must believe.

I have put together ten steps that I believe will facilitate a vision to those who are prepared to receive it:

STEP ONE

Have a purpose. Are you seeking answers regarding a particular question, topic, or problem? Have you sought it out and come to the conclusion that only the Lord can help you? This is an appropriate reason to seek a vision from the Lord.

STEP TWO

Get comfortable. Honestly, a vision can happen anywhere and anytime, but when going out of your way to seek a vision, it may be a good idea to sit down and relax. Relax your mind and body. Breathe deeply and remove the stresses that may inhibit the Lord's Spirit. I like to sit on the ground, but you can be most anywhere that it is quiet and where you can concentrate.

STEP THREE

Ask the Lord if you can shield yourself from the Adversary to prevent deception. If you hear the affirmative answer that a bad spirit is present, say in your mind, "In the name of Jesus Christ, by His authority, I command that a shield be placed around me to shield me from any unclean spirits that would try to deceive me or cause harm."[76] Ask the Lord if you did it correctly. I would suggest reviewing the chapter "Receiving Revelation." (pg. 29)

STEP FOUR

Ask the Lord if he will share a vision with you through His Spirit. Be specific and ask with faith. As with any revelation, you must pray for what you desire. I would suggest reviewing the section "Praying with Power." (pg. 39)

STEP FIVE

Be patient. It may take some effort on your part. We often expect the Lord to just drop it in our lap. When Lehi had his vision of the Tree of Life he had to wander in the wilderness of his mind for three hours before the vision unfolded.[77]

---

[76] The exact words are not important. As long as you do it in Jesus' name, by His authority, and are specific.

[77] 1 Nephi 8:8

Nephi sat pondering for an unknown amount of time and others often have to wait, but perhaps you won't.

STEP SIX

Begin the vision. Learn the art of visualization.[78] I'm only touching upon this here. Further in the book we spend a larger section on this topic.

Here is a simple exercise you can try: Visualize yourself, from your vantage point, walking up to a door. Try to see it as vividly as possible. Open the door and look where it leads. Do not be startled by what you see, do not retreat. Simply let this self-imposed vision go wherever it will. Continue to pray as you experience the vision. At some point, the Spirit will likely begin to control what you see and it will reveal the Lord's will to you. (This is explained in more detail on page 159.)

STEP SEVEN

Don't be hasty. Explore the surroundings of your vision. Look at details. Think of colors and smells and feelings. When there is nothing more there, look on, move forward, and keep asking.

STEP EIGHT

Immediately after your vision ask the Lord if it was from Him. Get a confirmation. You may already know it is, but perhaps only part of it was. If nothing happens it may be that you need to follow the steps on the "Praying with

---

[78] Hebrews 11:1

Power." It may be that your thoughts are too cumbered with stress, worry, or the Spirit hasn't been able to reach you for some reason. If you struggle, fasting may be the solution to open the door.

STEP NINE

Write down the vision. Think of as many details as possible. Remember feelings and impressions. Allow the Spirit to guide your writing. This is personal scripture to you. Much of what you will receive will be answers to direct prayer, prophecy of future events, and what the Lord wants you to understand about your mission.

STEP TEN

Express gratitude to the Lord in prayer. Review with Him what you have written. Ask Him if there is anything false in your writing. Ask if there is anything else he wants you to know and understand. Don't be surprised if another vision opens up to you. Expect the unexpected.

What is it like to have a vision? You might say its like recalling a movie you saw. Can you envision it in your mind? How clearly do you see the images? There are parts where you may only recall glimpses, and others where you can see the whole scene. A vision from the Lord will have clarity and you will feel the Spirit as it occurs. Sometimes the images may seem random and other times there is no doubt. You can see in different directions and are not limited to the confines of your body. The mind is capable of far more than we give it credit.

WHAT WOULD PREVENT YOU FROM HAVING A VISION?

1. Focusing upon frivolous things, e.g., TV/movies, sports, investments, work, and other facets of Babylon.
2. Unbelief because of learned reasoning regarding psychology, science, or past experiences.
3. Not taking your spiritual experiences serious, humor, sarcasm (mind must be firm in every form of godliness[79]).
4. Depression, heavy sorrow, anger, extreme emotion, guilt, and unforgiveness can sometimes prevent one from rending the veil, but not always.
5. Telling yourself the following: I don't have the gift of seeing or hearing; the Lord doesn't work with me or do things like this to me; not believing; lacking patience; having incessant negative chatter; becoming stressed that it is now or never.
6. Inability to focus and unwillingness to try and create the image in your mind for fear it could be just your own thoughts.
7. Fear of failure, the unknown, ridicule from friends or family, or embarrassment for being found out. You can get past all of this—just believe.

---

[79] Moroni 7:29-30

Receiving Angels
Chapter Eight

One of the things I love about the Book of Mormon is that it shows the pattern for receiving the gifts of the Spirit, including the gift of the ministering and beholding of angels.[80] It is my desire that each of you have the experience of receiving the ministering of angels and standing in the presence of the Savior that you may really know Him. Once this occurs, it will be a regular event in your life. If you truly have such a desire the Lord will manifest this gift to you.

> For it came to pass after I had desired to know the things that my father had seen, and believing that the Lord was able to make them known unto me, as I sat pondering in mine heart I was caught away in the Spirit of the Lord, yea, into an exceedingly high mountain, which I never had before seen, and upon which I never had before set my foot. (1 Nephi 11:1)

Nephi had a great desire to know the things his father Lehi had seen. What things in particular?[81] Lehi had seen the fate of Jerusalem, the throne of the Father, and perhaps many more things not recorded in the books of Nephi. Nephi wanted to see all that his father had seen and

---

[80] Moroni 10:14

[81] 1 Nephi 2:16, 1 Nephi 11:1

believed he could, as his father had undoubtedly told him this was possible for him.

Nephi sat pondering in his heart when he was caught away in the Spirit. What does it mean to ponder in your heart? I believe the heart is the part of the body where our spirit determines who we are as individuals. Here is where our desires, affections, and passions are felt. Nephi yearned for his God and to be close to Him. Under such circumstances, Nephi was taken to the exceedingly high mountain where he spoke with the angel.

All of us are capable of having visions and receiving Angels, as did Nephi and all of the prophets, if we will open our hearts to such things.

> For behold, they are subject unto him, to minister according to the word of his command, showing themselves unto them of strong faith and a firm mind in every form of godliness. And the office of their ministry is to call men unto repentance, and to fulfil and to do the work of the covenants of the Father, which he hath made unto the children of men, to prepare the way among the children of men, by declaring the word of Christ unto the chosen vessels of the Lord, that they may bear testimony of him. (Moroni 7:30, 31)

If your mind is firm and your faith is strong you are ready to receive them, but what can you do to facilitate this?

HOW TO RECEIVE AN ANGEL

Most people see this as a radical and presumptuous topic. Me, receive an angel? I don't remember reading about this in the Church Handbook. Would we be guilty of "seeking for a sign" if we entertained the idea? What do you think? How should we view the visitation of angels? Why was it okay for Nephi to seek visions and not us? Is it appropriate to "seek" these blessings now?

WHAT DOES MORONI SAY?

"And again, I exhort you, my brethren, that ye deny not the gifts of God, for they are many; and they come from the same God. And there are different ways that these gifts are administered; but it is the same God who worketh all in all; and they are given by the manifestations of the Spirit of God unto men, to profit them." (Moroni 10:8)

"And again, to another, the beholding of angels and ministering spirits;" (vs. 14)

"And now I speak unto all the ends of the earth—that if the day cometh that the power and gifts of God shall be done away among you, it shall be because of unbelief." (vs. 24)

"And again I would exhort you that ye would come unto Christ, and lay hold upon every good gift, and touch not the evil gift, nor the unclean thing." (vs. 30)

Moroni teaches that the beholding of angels is for our

profit. He exhorts us to lay hold on this gift.

WHAT IS AN ANGEL?

An angel is simply a being from beyond the veil that is on the Lord's assignment.[82] There are all kinds and each have different duties. Some are messengers and protectors with great glory from the Most High. Others are family and loved ones who watch over us. They are kind, they are loving, they are powerful, and they always want to help.

Part of coming unto Christ is to receive angels, but where do you start? Here are some things to consider that may make a difference for you.

THE STEPS TO RECEIVE AN ANGEL

1 Be believing. Cast away your doubts and expect the unexpected.
2 Ask the Lord (James 1:5). This is how you open the door. Ask the Lord to specifically send an Angel to administer to you. But remember, you must ask with real intent, nothing wavering.
3 Take time to be holy. Set aside some time to ponder, fast, pray, and prepare for instruction. You don't have to be perfect, but your thoughts need to be focused. Follow the four steps to praying with power.
4 Don't set limitations. You can ask for departed loved ones, people in the scriptures, notable past spirits. If

---

[82] Hebrews 1:14

the Lord permits it, they will come. This is not some kind of spiritualism. This is a gift of the Spirit that the Lord wishes to bestow upon each of us who desire and ask.

5 Be sure to check if they are a true messenger.[83] Usually asking the Lord is sufficient. The Adversary may try to deceive you; this is why it is good idea to shield the room and conversation before your prayer begins.

6 Don't be surprised if you only hear them first. You will begin by hearing a voice, which is unmistakable as the intelligence flows into your mind. Eventually you will see them in a vision as the Lord sees fit.

7 If the Angels are translated or withholding their glory they may appear as a regular person, but glory surrounding them can be felt. The Father and the Son appeared to Joseph in a vision. Yet Moroni came to Joseph as a translated being.[84] As they say, angels have

---

[83] D&C129:4-8

[84] There is no direct quote where Joseph Smith states whether Moroni was translated or resurrected. It states in the Introduction of the Book of Mormon (which was not written until 1981), " . . . Moroni, then a glorified, resurrected being, appeared to the Prophet Joseph Smith . . ." and according to a Deseret News article, *Debate renewed with change in Book of Mormon introduction*, Published in Nov. 8 2007, "The church declined comment on who wrote that version of the page." My personal revelation is that he was translated; but you should pray for your own revelation if it interests you.

visited people unawares.[85]

8 Always ask questions. They will bring a message, but if you don't ask questions you will miss a great opportunity.[86]
9 When they leave, thank the Lord and then ask if there is any other knowledge He wants you to have?
10 Record your experience in your personal journal. This is personal scripture that you will study and relish it in the future. Often Angels will come as you are writing, so this is a step not worth forgetting.

The same list that would prevent you from receiving a vision would also prevent you from having an Angel come to you.[87] Please, don't set stakes in the ground. Be open and believing and the Lord will bring you along as quickly as you are willing.

I talk about this in later chapters, but understand, when you see an angel don't expect to be blinded by their glory. You will see with your spiritual eyes, unless he or she appears without their glory as a translated being. With the spiritual eyes, in vision, they will be glorious and brilliant, but you will feel comfortable in their presence. You will know it is a real experience, because the clarity and fluidity of thought and communication will be sublime, invigorating, and sacred.

---

[85] Hebrews 13:2

[86] 3 Nephi 17:1-3

[87] This book, pg. 52

The Adversary

Chapter Nine

I have debated with myself as to how much information and detail to describe in these next few chapters on the Adversary. But this book is about how to have your Second Comforter; therefore, I feel that it is important to share as much as I can from my personal experience that may have an impact on helping you come to the Lord. I know this topic will cause some to feel uncomfortable, but it is important, because as you learn to face the Adversary you also learn about the realm of angels and God's glory.

I had a conversation with my son who recently returned from his mission. He said, "Why is it important to have to deal with bad spirits? It seems like the less I think about it the less it happens. If I just pray, read my scriptures, and have the Spirit, I'm okay." My response was that you can live like that and be fine, but the purpose of this is not for personal gain. When you become a servant of the Lord you can do more when you understand and confront the enemy. I have a stewardship over my family and there are times when I can bless them through the priesthood by knowing how to overcome the Adversary. This also extends to my other family members, my brothers and sisters, for we are all to be our brother's keeper (in the sense of caring for them, praying for them, showing forth charity), and therefore it can extend to the entire human family as long as God gives permission for us to act.

But there is more. Why do you think the Lord allows evil spirits to occupy this earth and bother us? Is it simply to keep them out of heaven, so they can't cause any mischief there?

> For it must needs be, that there is an opposition in all things. If not so, my firstborn in the wilderness, righteousness could not be brought to pass, neither wickedness, neither holiness nor misery, neither good nor bad. Wherefore, all things must needs be a compound in one; wherefore, if it should be one body it must needs remain as dead, having no life neither death, nor corruption nor incorruption, happiness nor misery, neither sense nor insensibility. (2 Nephi 2:11)

Part of our journey in coming to know the Savior is learning to overcome the Adversary. We must at some point confront him and have the courage and understanding to declare our allegiance to God and overcome any fear.[88] One cannot stand *confident* in the presence of God after having succumbed to temptation and fear of Satan.[89] If you cannot testify against Satan by trusting in God fully, the Adversary will prevent you from reaching your full potential.

---

[88] Psalms 23:4

[89] 1 John 4:18. A perfect love for the Lord implies trust in Him and helps us to overcome our fear of the Adversary.

"Joseph ... said the nearer a person approached to the Lord, the greater power would be manifest by the devil to prevent the accomplishment of the purposes of God." [90]

I am reminded of Moses, confronted by Satan before he was shown the vision of all things.

> And it came to pass that when Moses had said these words, behold, Satan came tempting him, saying: Moses, son of man, worship me. And it came to pass that Moses looked upon Satan and said: Who art thou? For behold, I am a son of God, in the similitude of his Only Begotten; and where is thy glory, that I should worship thee? For behold, I could not look upon God, except his glory should come upon me, and I were transfigured before him. But I can look upon thee in the natural man. Is it not so, surely? Blessed be the name of my God, for his Spirit hath not altogether withdrawn from me, or else where is thy glory, for it is darkness unto me? And I can judge between thee and God; [Moses, now by his own experience, can discern between God and Satan.] for God said unto me: Worship God, for him only shalt thou serve. Get thee hence, Satan; deceive me not; for God said unto me: Thou art after the similitude of mine Only Begotten. And he also gave me commandments when he called unto me out of the burning bush,

---

[90] President Heber C. Kimball's Journal: Seventh Book of the Faith-Promoting Series, Ch. 14

> saying: Call upon God in the name of mine Only Begotten, and worship me. And again Moses said: I will not cease to call upon God, I have other things to inquire of him: for his glory has been upon me, wherefore I can judge between him and thee. Depart hence, Satan.
>
> And now, when Moses had said these words, Satan cried with a loud voice, and ranted upon the earth, and commanded, saying: I am the Only Begotten, worship me. And it came to pass that Moses began to fear exceedingly; and as he began to fear, he saw the bitterness of hell. Nevertheless, calling upon God, he received strength, and he commanded, saying: Depart from me, Satan, for this one God only will I worship, which is the God of glory. [Moses experiences fear, but is given "strength" by which he learns how to overcome Satan.] And now Satan began to tremble, and the earth shook; and Moses received strength, and called upon God, saying: In the name of the Only Begotten, depart hence, Satan. And it came to pass that Satan cried with a loud voice, with weeping, and wailing, and gnashing of teeth; and he departed hence, even from the presence of Moses, that he beheld him not. (Moses 1:12-22)

What is interesting about this passage is that Satan came to Moses after he had seen the Lord. There are some that believe that the closer you come to the Lord, the less you will be tempted and experience the evil one.

Many will confront Satan long before they see the Lord. At the very beginning of Joseph Smith's journey he too had to deal with the Adversary.

> After I had retired to the place where I had previously designed to go, having looked around me, and finding myself alone, I kneeled down and began to offer up the desires of my heart to God. I had scarcely done so, when immediately I was seized upon by some power which entirely overcame me, and had such an astonishing influence over me as to bind my tongue so that I could not speak. Thick darkness gathered around me, and it seemed to me for a time as if I were doomed to sudden destruction.
>
> But, exerting all my powers to call upon God to deliver me out of the power of this enemy which had seized upon me, [Joseph's first lesson] and at the very moment when I was ready to sink into despair and abandon myself to destruction—not to an imaginary ruin, but to the power of some actual being from the unseen world, who had such marvelous power as I had never before felt in any being—just at this moment of great alarm, I saw a pillar of light exactly over my head, above the brightness of the sun, which descended gradually until it fell upon me. (Joseph Smith History 1:15-16)

Why did the Lord allow Joseph to experience such an

encounter with Satan? Was there a reason for this to occur? Is there a pattern?

Jesus Himself had a direct collision with Satan on the Mount of Temptation immediately after His baptism.

> And when the tempter came to him, he said, If thou be the Son of God, command that these stones be made bread. But he answered and said, It is written, Man shall not live by bread alone, but by every word that proceedeth out of the mouth of God. Then the devil taketh him up into the holy city, and setteth him on a pinnacle of the temple. And saith unto him, If thou be the Son of God, cast thyself down: for it is written, He shall give his angels charge concerning thee: and in their hands they shall bear thee up, lest at any time thou dash thy foot against a stone. Jesus said unto him, It is written again, Thou shalt not tempt the Lord thy God. Again, the devil taketh him up into an exceeding high mountain, and sheweth him all the kingdoms of the world, and the glory of them;
>
> And saith unto him, All these things will I give thee, if thou wilt fall down and worship me. Then saith Jesus unto him, Get thee hence, Satan: for it is written, Thou shalt worship the Lord thy God, and him only shalt thou serve. Then the devil leaveth him, and, behold, angels came and ministered unto him. (Matthew 4:3-11)

After Jesus resisted Satan, the angels came and ministered to Him. It is interesting that Jesus never became angry with Satan, but calmly rejected his temptations by quoting scripture.

This is good information, but until one has a personal experience with the Adversary it may seem as odd or strange as seeing an angel. These things don't happen to every-day folk.

I was in that camp of thinking until the Lord decided it was time to pop my bubble.

In the Spring of 2012 life seemed pretty good. Business is good, *check*, family is good, *check*, health is good, *check*. We're just happily waiting for the Second Coming to come, right?

But now our life was about to change. And at first what seemed to be a nightmare, became one of the greatest blessings of our lives.

It began as my wife had prayed and fasted, determined to overcome her fears of the Adversary. She had a traumatic childhood dealing with bad spirits and therefore had much fear of that kind of thing. She would not enter a dark room alone, and she felt that it was time to put this all behind her.

She explained to me that the Lord had told her by the Spirit that now was the time for her to overcome this fear. I was casually supportive, thinking to myself, "Good, she can get over this and we can move on." Little did I know I would be pulled into this in a way I couldn't have possibly imagined.

That night, as we both were sleeping, I heard a loud ringing in my ears, followed by a punch to my hip. My wife had hit me and begun shouting for me to wake up. At the very moment I was about to roll over, because of the ringing noise; a dark spirit had approached her on her side of the bed with a megaphone of sorts, yelling at her. It was a very real and tangible experience for both of us. The odd thing was that we experienced it together at the same time.

We began to experience, on a regular basis, strange things in the house. We would hear noises and see many things. The Lord told us to relax, pray, and that He would guide us through this. At first we would feel an uneasy presence, or hear sounds or words. Yes, at times what we experienced was creepy, but the Lord would always tell us what to do and it would go away.

I don't want this portion of the book to be overly detailed, but needless to say, the Lord taught us about how to deal with the Adversary in all his darkness. It would have been horrific if it hadn't been balanced by beings of light and the comfort of angels and what we learned in the process. I had never heard of anyone having this happen to them, let alone experience it together with their spouse at the same time. Even some of our children saw much of what was happening and we had to pray that the Lord would veil their eyes, because it was becoming too much of a distraction in their lives.

Our experiences escalated over the next two months. Things would seem as if they couldn't possibly be more crazy or intense and each consecutive night would beat all. It was always a different situation. We would both wake up, usually around 3:00 AM in the morning, and we would be given specific instructions for what to do and where to go in the house.[91] This is why we came to call it our "Training Camp," because the Lord was opening our eyes to not just the realm of the Adversary, but the realm of Heaven. We learned to use light and see how angels control the Adversary. It wasn't easy, and quite exhausting. My wife and I would sometimes experience things together, or be told to have one of us stay in the bedroom while the other go into another room or even outside the house. We usually were told to do things in the dark, but it was so beautiful. How could that be? We learned to hear the voice of the Lord as we would be told specifically what to do. Sometimes it would be like, "Take two steps, turn to your left, and then ..." We learned to discern the difference between the voice of the Lord and the voice of familiar spirits.[92] We learned about the realm of the Adversary, its complexities and nuances, and the Lord was with us. In the process, we grew to have no fear of Satan as we saw the power of God in our behalf. Satan's two biggest weapons he uses against us are

---

[91] We didn't wake ourselves. Usually it was a gentle awakening by the Spirit of the Lord. We always felt protected.

[92] A spirit that appears or sounds good to you, but has ill intent.

fear[93] and discouragement. The Lord uses the priesthood; and it can only be wielded with courage, love,[94] and according to His will.

Some might say it was a delusion or imaginary experience, but I know the difference. We saw and felt and heard things that we had never heard of before. Why would the Lord allow us to experience all this? Could it be to teach us the tangible reality of the spiritual realm? My wife and I kept all this to ourselves. We had nobody to talk with, let alone share what we experienced. They would think we were crazy.

When I now hear those that say they "hope they never encounter the Evil One," my answer is: You don't know what you are talking about! If you have the fortune of meeting Satan, not because of your own mistakes, but because God prepares it—rejoice, for you are about to begin a journey which will lead you into the presence of God. Not everyone who has their Second Comforter experiences the Adversary to the extent we did, but you will be taught so that you can discern the difference clearly.

---

[93] 2 Timothy 1:7

[94] 1 John 4:18

Know Your Enemy

Chapter Ten

The Adversary is not a random, keystone cop organization that throws small darts at us from time to time. It is an organized, sophisticated effort to break us down, destroy our families, and lead us out of the light.

"For we wrestle not against flesh and blood, but against principalities, against powers, against the rulers of the darkness of this world, against spiritual wickedness in high places." (Ephesians 6:12)

According to Paul, we must wrestle against the unseen realm. You must win the battle over Satan if you desire to have your Second Comforter experience. Not just to avoid temptation, but to cast him out of your presence. Is it not a good idea to know your enemy in order to better defeat them?

What is Satan's purpose? " . . . for he seeketh that all men might be miserable like unto himself." (2 Nephi 2:27) Satan considers himself the God of this world, and desires our allegiance and worship.[95] You are his greatest prize, but he knows he must tread carefully, for God has set his bounds[96] and he knows his antics can send you straight into the arms

[95] Moses 1:12

[96] Genesis 3:15

of the Savior if he pushes too hard. So, he stays his hand and often uses particular spirits to lull us into a sense of security, often deceiving us to think all is well and that these things are unrealistic.

> And others will he pacify, and lull them away into carnal security, that they will say: All is well in Zion; yea, Zion prospereth, all is well—and thus the devil cheateth their souls, and leadeth them away carefully down to hell. And behold, others he flattereth away, and telleth them there is no hell; and he saith unto them: I am no devil, for there is none—and thus he whispereth in their ears, until he grasps them with his awful chains, from whence there is no deliverance. (2 Nephi 28:21, 22)

I want to use the following pages to enlighten the reader concerning the realm of the Adversary. It is important to be aware of these things, as "knowledge is power," which is true of anything dealing with the unseen world.

There are four basic categories that exist with the Adversary:

1. Vagabond Spirits (disembodied spirits organized by the Adversary with specific tasks to afflict the Sons and Daughters of Light)
2. Dark Creatures (malicious creatures with many levels of intelligence and power who serve Satan)
3. Dark Spirits (pre-mortal spirits who followed Satan, Sons of Perdition)

4. Satan's Leadership (Teachers, Priests, Apostles, Presidency)

A mirror image of God's Kingdom exists, which with great organization, Satan strives to draw the Sons and Daughters of Light to him. Once you are prepared spiritually, the first step to winning the battle is to know your enemy.

I have found that of all of Satan's servants the most dangerous and deceitful are the most attractive, which is to say they appeal to our righteous sensibilities and are so subtle that they can even deceive the very Elect.[97] These are called "familiar spirits."[98] Such spirits are so familiar to us in the language they use that by means of flattery and attractive speech they endeavor to cause us to lose focus, to move our trajectory even one percent off course; for they know if they are successful they can ruin us.[99] They appeal to us by speaking lies that sound virtuous and even righteous, but is not the Lord's will. The closer one gets to the Lord, the more one has to deal with these kind. The Lord allows it, for in no other way can we more fully learn to

---

[97] Alma 30:53, Matthew 24:24

[98] Joseph Smith taught that without the priesthood and a knowledge of the laws by which spirits are governed, it is impossible to discover the difference between the miracles of Moses and the magicians of the pharaoh or between those of the apostles and Simon the sorcerer. (TPJS, pg. 202-206)

[99] Matthew 7:22-23

discern His voice from the imposter. Always check yourself and be sure your inspiration is from the right source.

TOOLS OF THE ADVERSARY

The Adversary is very organized in his work and has been for a long time. I have roughly described the four categories of Satan's minions, but many of us are unfamiliar with the means he uses to cause harm. Here is a short list of tools the Adversary will use against you:

MARKINGS

These are like graffiti written on buildings and property, and they are used to alert other spirits to what kind of sin is taking place there, what kind of spirits have taken residency there, or how the Adversary would like them to attack.

DEVICES

These are a kind of gadget that is attached to an object that projects negative thoughts or feelings that are harmful. Such devices can lead to depression, immorality, hate, lust, and all kinds of sin. They allow Satan to expand his influence. These can be attached to ANYTHING. Usually the Adversary chooses things that are gazed upon on a regular basis such as mirrors, wall hangings, decorations, books, the computer, etc.

PORTALS

These are used to bring certain bad spirits directly to the home. Once a portal is opened, the intensity of the conflict with the adversary increases. Like a doorway, spirits can easily move from place to place, a very common means of travel in the spirit realm.

ASSIGNED SPIRITS

There are spirits that are sent to accomplish specific things. They specialize in certain sins and will attach themselves to a victim if possible. Such spirits include these specialties: addiction, sickness, lust, anger, depression, hate, abuse, and doubt.

Each of these spirits can be cleaned away using the Lord's priesthood. Usually it requires the help of angels and you all have the right to ask for them if your heart is good with the Lord (ministering of angels[100]). As soon as the items are removed, the Adversary usually goes to work to try and restore what he has lost. Think of it as having your home sprayed for insects. It is clean for a short time and then has to be cleaned again regularly. I believe it is good to understand what we are up against in this fight. Our advantage is that we have the Spirit of the Lord to show us all things that we should do.[101]

Perhaps my definition of priesthood may be different than what you were taught. For me, it is whatever power or authority the Lord chooses to bestow upon you.[102] This is equally applicable to both men and women, even

---

[100] Omni 1:25, Moroni 7:29, Moroni 10:14

[101] 2 Nephi 32:5

[102] D&C 121:36-40

children.[103] By personal revelation, you can receive the authority to deal with the Adversary,[104] and in this way you may more fully come to understand the gift of revelation and how to hear the Lord clearly. It is a beautiful process that leads the seeker of knowledge into a fuller understanding of the heavenly realm.

As helpful as the before mentioned tools are to the Adversary, “fear and discouragement”[105] are his greatest tools to prevent us from overcoming him.[106] Most of us live a very passive lifestyle when dealing with the enemy. We suppose that almost all ills we suffer are just the natural consequences of life. Actually, things such as sickness, depression, anxiety, and other ailments can at times be rooted in the influence of the Adversary. The Lord allows him to afflict us so that we can overcome and learn the lessons of mortality. Satan has his way with us and only when we repent and come unto Christ are we released momentarily from these chains.[107] At times we are given adversity so that we can learn to demonstrate faith and overcome in His name. [108]

Many people simply ignore Satan because they think he’s such a puny weakling, that he can do no harm to them, and that they will be protected. This is false. There is no place

---

[103] Alma 32:23, Psalms 8:2

[104] 2 Peter 1:3

[105] Romans 8:15

[106] 2 Timothy 1:7

[107] John 5:14, Matthew 9:5-6

[108] John 9:3

on this earth he will not go, or person he will not attack.[109] If you think that hanging pictures of Jesus or the temple on your walls will deter him, you are mistaken. You can play Mormon Tabernacle Choir music all day long and it will do nothing, except maybe irritate them a little.[110] In my experiences with the Adversary, no shield has ever been permanent[111] and the only time I've ever been 100% free without concern is when I was on the "High Mountain" or in the presence of the Lord.[112] (This is explained in later chapters.)

TOOLS WE CAN USE AGAINST THE ADVERSARY

The Lord has set boundaries that the Adversary cannot pass[113] and will teach his servants how to control him, but we must trust in the Lord implicitly. Remember, there is no power within ourselves to do anything of our own, only by the authority He bestows upon us. Our idea of priesthood is convoluted if we think the Adversary has any fear of us. Only in the manifestation of God's power do they withdraw.

Here is a brief list of the most common tools YOU will learn to use under the Lord's direction:

---

[109] Job 1:7, Job 2:2

[110] If the music inspires you to pray and seek the Lord it is good, but the music in itself does not deter the Adversary.

[111] Moses 7:26 (Attitude of Satan)

[112] Alma 34:36, 1 Nephi 10:21, Exodus 3:1-15

[113] D&C 122:7-9

REVELATION

This is the most important tool we use in confronting any kind of evil. Each situation is different. Ask the Lord what you should do and learn to hear His voice as you are instructed. You have to be quick on your feet when dealing with these things, and the Lord will sometimes allow the Adversary to confront you to give you experience so that you can develop your Spiritual Gifts. Ask the Lord to give you that which will help you to serve others and draw closer to Him.

SHIELDS

Building on step one, shielding is a critical part of dealing with the Adversary. These can be quickly applied, with the Lord's permission and can protect or veil yourself and others from harm. They are not permanent and it may be wise to ask how long it will last. The shield is created by the Lord's light and power and can be seen by the Adversary. It angers these bad spirits and in some cases frightens them.

CALLING DOWN ANGELS

Usually, the Lord will allow you to call down Angels of Light, Soldiers of the Most High, to remove the bad spirits. They will usually only do that which they have been instructed to do, so you need to be specific. Angels have different purposes. Some are sent to deal with the Adversary; others are sent to comfort, to bless, to prepare the way. Some are sent to observe only. Some angels are very large and powerful, while others are small and gentle. Some angels are friends and family who have departed or have not yet come to mortality. It is appropriate to ask the Lord who they are and why they are here.[114] Sometimes the answers you get when asking them directly are surprising. Each Angel has a unique personality and many of them know you better than your best friend, because in actuality they are your best friend and associated with you in heaven.

CORDS OF LIGHT

I was surprised when I learned of this. When the Lord gives you permission, you can control His light. There are occasions in confronting the Adversary or his minions when you can ask that cords of light bind them. Often when dealing with more than your typical vagabond or dark spirit these cords can stop a dangerous situation. The Lord will instruct you when to use them. Often you may be instructed in a creative manner on how to do this. After these bad spirits are bound they are usually escorted away by angels to another place.

SYMBOLS

There are specific symbols that have eternal meaning that the Adversary will respond to immediately. When the Lord commands it, as given to you by revelation, you do it. Examples would be the arm to the square, feet and hand gestures and voice volume.

PORTALS

This was a surprise to me when I first learned of it by the Lord. Perhaps it is one of the most common and ordinary forms of travel among those not confined to our mortality.

---

[114] Genesis 32:29

A portal can be created almost anywhere and is used by both the Adversary and angelic hosts. Sometimes a portal needs to be opened and at other times shut. They are a useful way to quickly put away bad spirits under the Lord's direction.

ETERNAL FLAME

This is not the kind of fire that we think of; this is the glory of the Lord that, when used under His direction, will clean and remove all unclean items within its path. As the Lord directs, it will sweep out an area or move the Adversary away. Usually it is used as more of a warning to them.

ARMOR

Another item I was somewhat surprised to learn is that spiritual armor is more than a metaphor. At some point your armor will be placed upon you as you gain power in battling the Adversary. I believe it is the same armor we had before we came into our mortal bodies. The armor is a sign of your glory and standing with the Lord, but also prevents the Adversary from doing bodily damage to you. It will protect you from unclean spirits who would afflict you with sickness, depression, or other types of possession. It will also give you strength to fight temptation. You must be careful that you veil your light in public or you will have a hoard of bad spirits follow you home. To learn more about this, I would suggest praying for revelation on the subject. (I will cover this more fully in the coming chapter.)

When my wife and I experienced these things we came closer to the Lord and learned of the Gifts of the Spirit more than any other way. It was like a crash course in how to receive revelation, confront the Adversary on the Lord's terms, and the manifestations of His power. We did not seek these things out of curiosity or sign seeking. I trust that the Lord only gives us as much as we are able to bear. You may want to ask the Lord what further light and knowledge you need with regard to this topic.

LOVE

The way you feel in your heart as you battle the Adversary has much to do with the degree of your success. If you have any feelings of anger, pride, or fear, you will only strengthen the opposing force. It is also important to understand that true charity doesn't mean that you don't mete out justice when it is called for, or back away for fear of hurting them and being un-Christlike. We confront the devil as a servant of the Lord with so much love for God that we feel no fear– "for pure love casteth out all fear." When you are filled with this love your power against the Adversary is like the Lord's blinding light that penetrates all darkness.

MORE ABOUT SHEILDS

I used to think I could put my arm to the square and clean a house using my Melchizedek Priesthood, and I could not only scare away the bad spirits, but somehow create a shield that could never go away, unless somebody did something truly heinous.

When we went through our "Training Camp," the Lord taught us about using shields. When we started out, I had to go through a learning curve. Usually we would ask for a shield of light to cover us, or angels to stand guard around the house, and these shields only lasted for the night or a short time. I asked the Lord why they couldn't remain permanent and it was explained to me that this would not be beneficial for me if it did; that was not the answer I wanted to hear. After a while we found that certain shields were better than others and then the Lord began to teach us more and more. I won't go into that here, but I will say that the Lord will instruct you in this as you need to learn.

A typical prayer might be, "Lord, wilt thou shield me from the Adversary that I may be protected, or speak with thee without deception?" Then, it is good to check and ask the Lord if a shield has been applied. [115] I would even ask for how long it will remain active, because rarely are these shields permanent.

Keep in mind that there are many times when you do not need a shield other than your armor or light. Someone can become obsessed with this to the degree that it becomes a hindrance. It is best to check with the Lord to know when, where, and how often you should use this protection.

WHEN JESUS CAST OUT SPIRITS

---

[115] Refer to pg. 29 to review how to decipher revelations.

Jesus dealt with the Adversary throughout his ministry and taught His disciples how they could also cast out bad spirits. Here is an example from the life of the Savior as a man brought his son to Him who was possessed by an evil spirit.

> And wheresoever he taketh him, he teareth him: and he foameth, and gnasheth with his teeth, and pineth away: and I spake to thy disciples that they should cast him out; and they could not. He answereth him, and saith, O faithless generation, how long shall I be with you? how long shall I suffer you? bring him unto me. [His disciples had just tried to rebuke the unclean spirits and had failed. Was Christ disappointed in their faith regarding this thing? Had He not taught them? Would they have tried to cast out the spirit had they not been instructed?]
>
> And they brought him unto him: and when he saw him, straightway the spirit tare him; and he fell on the ground, and wallowed foaming. And he asked his father, How long is it ago since this came unto him? [Jesus asked the father for some history about his son's condition.] And he said, Of a child. And ofttimes it hath cast him into the fire, and into the waters, to destroy him: but if thou canst do any thing, have compassion on us, and help us.
>
> Jesus said unto him, If thou canst believe, all things are possible to him that believeth. And straightway the father of the child cried out, and said with

tears, Lord, I believe; help thou mine unbelief. [It's important that Jesus spoke these words for not only the father, but for the disciples to understand, and Jesus waited for the father to ask for help, and the father's response echoes the desire of His disciples.]

When Jesus saw that the people came running together, he rebuked the foul spirit, saying unto him, Thou dumb and deaf spirit, I charge thee, come out of him, and enter no more into him. [Jesus gave very specific instructions to the unclean spirit.] And the spirit cried, and rent him sore, and came out of him: and he was as one dead; insomuch that many said, He is dead. But Jesus took him by the hand, and lifted him up; and he arose.

And when he was come into the house, his disciples asked him privately, Why could not we cast him out? [Had the disciples discussed the topic with Jesus before? Most likely, yes. They expected to be able to deal with unseen spirits by His power.]

And he said unto them, This kind can come forth by nothing, but by prayer and fasting. (Mark 9:18-29)

The Lord gave further instructions: prayer (to seek for answers and power) and fasting (to help them receive open revelation).

The disciples were weak as to the principle of revelation and did not know the particulars for how to deal with spirit possession. There is not a one-size-fits-all method to deal with the Adversary, and without the spirit of revelation to guide us we may fail, as did Jesus' disciples. This scripture adds great insight into the Lord's dealing with Satan's realm and what the Lord expects of us.

I know that my experience with the Adversary is unique. Not everyone that has their Second Comforter will see all these things, but count yourself fortunate if you do. The glorious benefits outweigh the bad and the Lord will be with you each step of the way.

Armor of the Lord and the Light of God

Chapter Eleven

The Servants of God are beings of light and power. If an army of Satan's worst spirits were to come for you, would you be confident that you were prepared and protected? There are two things that will protect you from such a scenario. One is a sure knowledge that you are in tune with the spirit of revelation and are following the Lord's will. The second is a knowledge of what you are doing in relation to your protections, tools, and defenses against the Adversary.

This second piece of knowledge is the topic of this section. The Apostle Paul said the following:

> Finally, be strong in the Lord and in his mighty power. Put on the full armor of God, [not just a part of it] so that you can take your stand against the devil's schemes. For our struggle is not against flesh and blood, but against the rulers, against the authorities, against the powers of this dark world and against the spiritual forces of evil in the heavenly realms." [This scripture gives us a clue to the organization of Satan's realm. The armor is not just for looks or a fun metaphor.]
>
> Therefore put on the full armor of God, so that when the day of evil comes, you may be able to

> stand your ground, and after you have done everything, to stand. [There will be a time appointed to battle the Adversary.]
>
> Stand firm then, with the belt of truth buckled around your waist, with the breastplate of righteousness in place, and with your feet fitted with the readiness that comes from the gospel of peace. In addition to all this, take up the shield of faith, with which you can extinguish all the flaming arrows of the evil one. Take the helmet of salvation and the sword of the Spirit, which is the word of God. And pray in the Spirit on all occasions with all kinds of prayers and requests. With this in mind, be alert and always keep on praying for all the Lord's people." (Ephesians 6:10-18 NIV) [It says all kinds of prayers and requests—for what purpose? To protect the righteous people from the Adversary.]

Do you think this is a figurative scripture, or literal? Both my wife and I received our spiritual armor and we can tell you it is quite literal. I know it sounds strange, but each of us, during our "Training Camp" in dealing with the Adversary were given armor of light to help us to overcome his advances. This was given to us after we learned some of the basics of shielding and it was a great strength and comfort to our confidence. Again, do not be fearful as you read about this; the Lord was in control the entire time. He gave us a measured portion of the Adversary experience and we learned step by step how to identify, confront, and overcome these bad spirits. It was not a random and unmeasured encounter with the Adversary. In fact, the entire experience was holy, because the Lord was right there with us and his angels too. I hope each of you can experience this for yourself.

My wife and I received our armor at different times. She was the first to see this in vision and have it explained to her. She was given the following revelation:

> The "Helmet of Salvation" means to save or make safe, and stands for spiritual protection. It is a vital part of your armor. It gives you the power to control your thoughts and actions. Evil spirits try to enter into the crown of your head with all manner of devices or spiritual powers.
>
> The "Shield of Faith" gives you the strength to stand against your foes or enemies. It represents your faith in the Savior and the courage to do His will as a servant. It shines the brightest of all your armor pieces. It deflects or defeats the fiery darts of the Adversary. This is the testimony of your faith as you stand as a witness of Jesus Christ.
>
> The "Sword of Truth" is used for piercing the heart of both the living and the dead with the word of God. It uses your words with more power than words alone, because it pierces the heart and the soul of the spirits in whom you stand against as a witness of all you believe. As you speak words of

truth it pierces them to the very core and your testimony will stand as a witness against them at the last Day of Judgment. They "feel" the sword's power along with the words of truth, and it causes them to shrink and shudder.
The "Breastplate of Righteousness" protects you against their swords, and causes their words to be unable to pierce your heart.

The "Shoes" represent the destruction of the Adversary. They destroy his interference in your path by symbolizing the crushing of the serpent's head. The shoes are the last piece of armor you will use to defeat your enemies. The last step of battle is you will push your enemy down to Hell.[116] If the Spirit tells you to, stomp your feet three times, symbolizing it is finished. This is a witness and testimony of the battle in which you have fought. The shoes are also a symbol of your willingness to live and share the Gospel and your testimony to every person you encounter.

[End of Vision]

WHAT ARE THE FIERY DARTS?

"And I said unto them that it was the word of God; and whoso would hearken unto the word of God,

---

[116] This seems to create a portal that takes them away and/or seals up an existing portal.

> and would hold fast unto it, they would never perish; **neither could the temptations and the fiery darts of the adversary overpower them** unto blindness, to lead them away to destruction." (1 Nephi 15:24)

Temptations are real, so why not the fiery darts? What do they do? They weaken our resolve and our faith by placing doubts and fears upon us.

> For, behold, you should not have feared man more than God. Although men set at naught the counsels of God, and despise his words—Yet you should have been faithful; and he would have extended his arm and supported you **against all the fiery darts of the adversary**; and he would have been with you in every time of trouble.
>
> Behold, thou art Joseph, [you could insert your name here] and thou wast chosen to do the work of the Lord, but because of transgression, if thou art not aware thou wilt fall. (D&C 3:7-9)

What can we learn from this scripture? We need to always be aware of the fiery darts of the Adversary. If we are guilty of transgression, we may be clouded to the extent that we cannot hear the voice of the Lord. What are these fiery darts? I believe they come in the form of temptation, doubts, fear, wicked or evil thoughts, and even physical harm.

DO YOU HAVE YOUR ARMOR?

At some point in your spiritual journey the Lord will place armor upon you. It is seen only by the spiritual eyes and is a great gift to the righteous.

The armor comes with a calling. Sometimes we are given the armor we wore before we came to this earth and sometimes it is new. It bears light and prevents the Adversary from harming you, but one may still fall to temptation if not vigilant. Each of you should pray and ask about your armor. If you do not have it yet, you can pray and ask for it to be given to you, if it is the Lord's will.[117]

How is it given? An appointed angel of the Most High reverently places the armor upon you in a vision. Each piece has significance and a covenant. If these covenants are kept, the armor never leaves you. If broken it is removed. It is glorious and each is unique in beauty.

"Ask and it shall be given, knock and it shall be opened unto you."[118] You must pray and ask that your armor be given to you. Seek and allow the vision to present itself.

---

[117] Receiving armor can come by revelation unexpectedly, or by asking the Lord if it be His will. Often, all the Lord is waiting for is that we ask.

[118] 3 Nephi 14:7

THE LIGHT OF GOD

What is the Light of God and how is that relevant to what we just talked about?

"And God said, 'Let there be light,' and there was light. God saw that the light was good, and he separated the light from the darkness." (Genesis 1:3,4)

Light is a tangible thing that the Lord separates and uses for His purposes.

"I form the light and create darkness, . . ."[119] It is an act of creation and faith and by word that God forms his creations.

I have learned from experience that when we have the Lord's permission we can create things with light that are hardly imaginable. As mentioned in the previous section, things such as portals, shields, cords, walls of flame, and various weapons of light can be used to fight against the Adversary. Also, our very armor is made of light. This is only the beginning; I believe there is far more that we can learn.

"The light of the body is the eye: if therefore thine eye be single, [to the glory of God] thy whole body shall be full of light."[120] It is interesting that the word "eye" is used and not "eyes" in the King James Version. Our pineal gland is often

---

[119] Isaiah 45:7
[120] Matt 6:22

referred to as the third eye, and this is where we see beyond our normal senses. To view beyond the veil you must literally see what your mortal eyes cannot. We hardly have the science to understand the physiology of the human brain, let alone the spirit. There is much that can be strengthened in the mind by practice. Learning to see can be improved with practice.

> In the beginning was the Word, and the Word was with God, and the Word was God. The same was in the beginning with God. All things were made by him; and without him was not any thing made that was made. In him was life; and the life was the light of men. And the **light shineth in darkness; and the darkness comprehended it not**. (John 1:1-5)

In mortality most of us are in darkness to things of the spirit. The unseen realm is incomprehensible, but it is all around us if we will allow ourselves to see. We begin to see when we ask for the scales to be removed. Ask to receive your armor. Ask how to use it. Ask when it is appropriate to use it. Ask, ask, ask.

> And the light which shineth, which giveth you light, is through him who enlighteneth your eyes, which is the same light that quickeneth your understandings; Which light proceedeth forth from the presence of God to fill the immensity of space. The light which is in all things, which giveth life to all things, which is the law by which all things are governed, even the power of God who sitteth

> upon his throne, who is in the bosom of eternity, who is in the midst of all things. (D&C 88:11-13)

This glorious light is what opens our eyes to see through the veil and behold visions; and it quickens our understanding through revelation; it creates, governs, and is the very power and authority of God.

> For the word of the Lord is truth, and whatsoever is **truth is light**, and whatsoever is light is Spirit, even the Spirit of Jesus Christ. And the Spirit giveth light to every man that cometh into the world; and **the Spirit enlighteneth every man through the world, that hearkeneth to the voice of the Spirit. And every one that hearkeneth to the voice of the Spirit cometh unto God, even the Father.** (D&C 84:45-47)

If you learn to hearken to this light you will have your Second Comforter. Light means many different things by definition. It is truth, glory, and power. It is also the frequency of energy by which all things are created. When one has the sealing power, one can control all things by use of this light, which is the higher priesthood of God.[121] It is used to rebuke the Adversary, and to heal, protect, travel, learn, bless, or provide any other spiritual and physical gift the Lord sees fit to bestow upon us. That light obeys God's chosen vessels, because they are one with the Father, the Son, and the Holy Ghost.

---

[121] Helaman 10:4-11

Learning to handle the Adversary requires a careful walk with God, in all holiness, as you strive to do His will in all things. You become the apprentice of the master as you learn to do battle with the forces of evil in the unseen realms.

When you have a private moment, ask God about your armor. To be a servant of the Lord in the truest sense, you must be suited up for battle. Remember that this is not something to feel pride in, for we receive such gifts only for the benefit of serving our brothers and sisters. We are preparing to be His soldiers of light, and it will be glorious!

Baptism of Fire
Chapter Twelve

Joseph Smith taught, "The baptism of water, without the baptism of fire and the Holy Ghost attending it, is of no use, they are necessarily and inseparably connected. An individual must be born of water and the spirit in order to get into the kingdom of God." [122]

In the midst of learning many new things regarding revelation, angels, and the feeling of the Spirit being poured out upon me, I asked the fateful question, "Lord, have I had my Baptism of Fire?" I was sure I knew the answer, but had to ask anyway. I remembered many years ago, at the age of twelve, asking the Lord if Joseph was a prophet and feeling an overwhelming feeling of warmth and love flow over my body. My testimony felt secure, so I knew that experience had to be the moment. To my great surprise, the Lord said, "No, you have not had your Baptism of Fire yet."

What! How could this be? I was confused; what must I do to receive this Gift?

> And ye shall offer for a sacrifice unto me a broken

---

[122] History of the Church, 6:316; from a discourse given by Joseph Smith on Apr. 7, 1844, in Nauvoo, Illinois; reported by Wilford Woodruff, Willard Richards, Thomas Bullock, and William Clayton.

> heart and a contrite spirit. And whoso cometh unto me with a broken heart and a contrite spirit, him will I baptize with fire and with the Holy Ghost, even as the Lamanites, because of their faith in me at the time of their conversion, were baptized with fire and with the Holy Ghost, and they knew it not. (3 Ne. 9: 20)

There is something critical about having a broken heart and a contrite spirit if one wishes to qualify for their baptism of fire and to eventually have their Second Comforter experience.[123] What does a broken heart and contrite spirit mean? There are many interpretations, but for me it means this: If your heart is broken, you do not seek your own needs, but that of others, according to the Lord's will (full submission).[124] If your spirit is contrite, you are in a constant state of repentance, meaning that your heart is turned to God (full repentance). If these two attributes of godliness are within you, you shall be redeemed from the fall, be given the Gift of the Holy Ghost, have your baptism of fire, and be quickly on your way to having your Second Comforter experience.

Jesus Christ was in every way the perfect example for us of how to live our lives. A man without sin, He lived His entire life with a broken heart and a contrite spirit, as evidenced

---

[123] 2 Nephi 2:7

[124] You could also say that it means one is teachable of the Lord. The opposite of a broken heart is a hard heart, which is pride.

by His complete submission to His Father.[125]

Jesus said to His disciples, "Learn of me; for I am meek and lowly in heart."[126] In time, the perfect Lamb willingly laid His life upon the altar according to His Father's will, and partook of the bitter cup. God is looking for those who will be like Him, to take His name upon themselves, as is the promise in the Sacrament Prayer, that they may always have His Spirit to be with them.[127] This is the covenant[128] He desires to make with us, to give us the promise of the Gift of the Holy Ghost and the Baptism of Fire! If we are willing to submit to all He asks of us, as did He to His Father's will, we are worthy of the Gift.

The very essence of a broken heart and a contrite spirit is a desire to seek the Lord more than anything else in our life. When our hearts are broken, we understand the full measure of what it means to have charity,[129] which includes loving as Christ would love. By this we do His will in all things and we demonstrate His pure love to others. When we acquire this godly attribute, the Lord can make us greater than ourselves and we can fulfill the commandment: "Ye should be perfect even as I, or your Father who is in Heaven is perfect."[130]

---

[125] John 6:38
[126] Matthew 11:29
[127] Moroni 4:3, 5:2
[128] John 14:16
[129] Moroni 7:46-48
[130] 3 Nephi 12:48

> If so, his faith and hope is vain, for none is acceptable before God, save the meek and lowly in heart; and if a man be meek and lowly in heart, and confesses by the power of the Holy Ghost that Jesus is the Christ, he must needs have charity; for if he have not charity he is nothing; wherefore he must needs have charity.
>
> And charity suffereth long, and is kind, and envieth not, and is not puffed up, seeketh not her own, is not easily provoked, thinketh no evil, and rejoiceth not in iniquity but rejoiceth in the truth, beareth all things, believeth all things, hopeth all things, endureth all things.
>
> Wherefore, my beloved brethren, if ye have not charity, ye are nothing, for charity never faileth. Wherefore, cleave unto charity, which is the greatest of all, for all things must fail—
>
> But charity is the pure love of Christ, and it endureth forever; and whoso is found possessed of it at the last day, it shall be well with him. (Moroni 7:44-47)

It is important to understand that charity, "the pure love of Christ," is often misconstrued to mean to love *like* Christ,[131]

---

[131] Charity is a divine attribute of loving obedience that leads to acts of kindness and service, but also moments of conflict; e.g., cutting off the head of Laban, and Abraham

when it is better explained as a pure love *as* Christ. "Jesus answered and said unto him, if a man love me, he will keep my words: and my Father will love him, and we will come unto him, and make our abode with him." (John 14:23) If you develop a broken heart and a contrite spirit, with the pure love of Christ (charity), you will be ready to receive your baptism of fire and Second Comforter.

During this time of study, I researched more about the Baptism of Fire and wrote the following:

> When we receive our Baptism of Fire. We become holy and become a new person,[132] a "higher self," quickened in the Spirit. This increase in light enables us to speak with the tongue of angels,[133] to be holy and have an abundance of the Lord's Spirit with us always. We then are given the mysteries of godliness as the doctrines of the priesthood distill upon our souls as the dews of Heaven.[134] When we receive the Gift of the Holy Ghost, we also receive the Baptism of Fire.[135] You are claimed by Christ as His, and thereby are

---

being commanded to sacrifice his son. These are acts of righteousness that could not be accomplished without charity.

[132] 2 Corinthians 5:17

[133] 2 Nephi 31:13

[134] D&C 121:45

[135] Luke 3:16

> promised exaltation if you endure to the end.[136] All those who become exalted become "one with Christ and the Father." "Which Father, Son, and the Holy Ghost are one God," (D&C 20:28)[137] "If ye are not one, ye are not mine." (D&C 38:27)

This is the Godhead and the Holy Ghost is a part of that Eternal light and truth.[138] We must become one with Christ by receiving the Gift of the Holy Ghost and the Baptism of Fire.

How many of us have actually received the Gift of the Holy Ghost and the Baptism of Fire? Many assume that the words spoken by the priesthood holder at the time of the Confirmation is the moment they finally have the Gift of Holy Ghost. He says to the newly baptized person as the ordinance is given, "I confirm you a member of The Church of Jesus Christ of Latter-day Saints and say unto you, 'Receive the Holy Ghost.' " This is more an invitation to a future event than a declaration that they now have the Gift.

There are two ways to receive the Gift of the Holy Ghost and the Baptism of Fire. One is by the laying on of hands by the Lord's anointed Apostles[139] and the other is by the Lord Himself.[140] And when we say "the Lord's anointed," we

---

[136] 2 Nephi 31:18-20

[137] 3 Nephi 11:35-37

[138] John 17:21-23, 2 Nephi 31:21

[139] 3 Nephi 18:36-37, Moroni 2:2

[140] Moses 6:64-65, Acts 2:1-4

mean personally anointed by the Savior and not ordained by man.

It is not until we are found sufficiently prepared that we receive the Gift of the Holy Ghost and the Baptism of Fire and become sanctified and holy.

WHAT IS IT LIKE TO HAVE YOUR BAPTISM OF FIRE?

The Lord points out when He came to the Nephites in Bountiful that the Lamanites received the baptism of fire and were completely unaware of it.[141] In the Book of Helaman we read the story and gain some interesting insights of what occurs when one receives their Baptism of Fire. This great blessing came to them at the last second, when they needed it most, both physically and spiritually.

> And it came to pass that they all did begin to cry unto the voice of him who had shaken the earth; yea, they did cry even until the cloud of darkness was dispersed. And it came to pass that when they cast their eyes about, and saw that the cloud of darkness was dispersed from overshadowing them, [Similar to what Joseph Smith experienced in the grove.] behold, they saw that they were encircled about, yea every soul, by a pillar of fire. And Nephi and Lehi were in the midst of them; yea, they were encircled about; yea, they were as if in

---

141 3 Nephi 9:20

the midst of a flaming fire, yet it did harm them not, neither did it take hold upon the walls of the prison; and they were filled with that joy which is unspeakable and full of glory. And behold, the Holy Spirit of God did come down from heaven, and did enter into their hearts, and they were filled as if with fire, and they could speak forth marvelous words. (Helaman 5:42-45)

THE BAPTISM OF FIRE HAS SIX CHARACTERISTICS:

1. An encircling fire or pillar of fire, like a column of light or plasma that surrounds them.[142]
2. The presence and ministration of angels.[143]
3. A remission of sins.[144]
4. Purification of the heart by fire.[145]
5. Speaking with a new tongue (speaking the word of angels by the power of the Holy Ghost).[146]
6. Sanctification, or becoming holy, by being filled with the Holy Ghost.[147]

Why are there so few who have received their Baptism of Fire?

---

[142] Acts 2:1-4

[143] 3 Nephi 17:24

[144] 2 Nephi 31:17

[145] D&C 88:74

[146] 2 Nephi 32:2-3

[147] Alma 13:11-12

1. Is it because of unbelief in the Gifts of the Spirit as spoken by Moroni?[148]
2. Is it because their hearts are not sufficiently humble and contrite?
3. Is it a lack of faith, knowledge, or believing; they simply don't know?
4. Is it because they take the covenant of the Book of Mormon lightly?[149] (To literally "come unto Christ."[150])
5. Could it be that people are putting their trust in man instead of God?
6. Could it simply be that the appropriate time for many individuals has not yet occurred?

HOW I RECEIVED MY BAPTISM OF FIRE

To my benefit, I had made some close associations with some brothers starting at the beginning of 2015. We would meet together, share testimony and scripture, and discuss the things of the Spirit. We made plans to go up to the mountains together on June 20th, the day before the Summer Solstice, to pray and seek the Lord. Who knows, maybe something special would happen?

We hiked up to about 10,000 feet and found a beautiful secluded spot. Because we each wanted to spend the evening seeking the Lord, each of us brought our own

---

[148] Moroni 10:24
[149] D&C 84:54
[150] Moroni 10:32

private tent. I had decided to spend the entire evening praying, like Enos in the Book of Mormon. My plan was to spend the night expressing gratitude and praying for as many people as I could. I brought my hymnbook to help me. All night the wind blew so hard I thought my tent was under attack! I thought about the first Apostles and how they must have felt when they were on the tiny fishing boat on the Sea of Galilee being tossed to and fro by the storm while Jesus slept—the boat about to sink.

PERSONAL JOURNAL – JUNE 21, 2015

I heard the Voice of the Lord as I was in my tent that night. It came very clearly. In the midst of the wind blowing loudly around my tent, I heard a clear calming Voice say, "Tomorrow you will have your Baptism of Fire." After many hours of praying, and praising, and loving my Lord—I felt peace. I was about to go to sleep when three brothers tapped on my tent. They asked if they could give me a blessing. We walked a short distance from the tent and in the night air with the gusts of wind around us, I knelt, and each took a turn offering me a blessing. Wonderful gifts were promised in the name of the Lord. As this was happening my eyes were opened and I saw a clear and vivid vision.

An angel approached me and stood about three feet from me. He was magnificent. His hair was to his shoulders and appeared golden, but I'm not sure, as it could have been the light from his glory. What impressed me the most was his smile and manly features. He walked toward me and gave me something. I feel that I am not supposed to share that part, but it was amazing.

The next morning we gathered and prayed, sang hymns, and watched the sun rise. Many blessings were offered and the spirit of love and unity was powerful.

We were all standing together looking out at the morning vista when it happened. I looked up toward the sky and heard what sounded like angels singing. I listened again and the sound grew louder. I was gazing toward the source of the singing when the heavens opened; I saw many angels gathered in great light and then another layer parted and I saw what appeared to be the throne of God. He was there. My heart felt that it would burst with emotion and at that moment I felt a warm sensation come over me like oil being poured over my head. It then filled my heart and my whole body felt the power of the Lord and His love. The emotion and love and gratitude I felt at that moment were beyond description. I shouted out praises to God with all my heart.

After I had come to myself again I wiped the tears off my face. My body felt exhausted, but good. I asked the Lord, "Did I just receive the Baptism of Fire?" — "Yes!"

I looked around and was so happy to see everyone wrapped up in the Spirit as I was. Many were crying and on their knees. I felt that each brother was receiving according to his faith. I looked back again at the brothers; this time I noticed what looked like a white flame spinning atop many of the brothers' heads. I wondered if this had to be the cloven tongues of fire spoken in the scriptures. The whole experience was electrifying.

WHAT CAN YOU DO TO HAVE YOUR BAPTISM OF FIRE?

In retrospect I see that this as the most important experience I had leading to my Second Comforter. In many ways, for me, it was like a trial run for the time in which I would part the veil and have a close and personal experience with the Savior. What did I do right that day? I have talked to others who have had their Baptism of Fire and many were simply filled with the Holy Ghost and a feeling of total love and devotion when it occurred. In the end, it is good to pray and ask for sure whether you have received this important ordinance. In retrospect, here are a few things I did that helped me have this experience:

1. I wanted nothing more in the world than to come to my Lord. (Full submission.)
2. I carefully planned an entire day to make myself holy for Him, knowing full well that I would be blessed. But at the same time I didn't know how.
3. I fasted from food and sleep.
4. I did an Enos prayer all night, praying vocally. Because I didn't want to run out of things to pray about, I carefully prepared many pages of notes to help guide me. I brought my hymnbook to sing and praise.
5. I took the Sacrament. (More about this in next chapter.)

6. I made an oath that I would serve Him with all my heart.
7. I was praying and thinking and encouraging the others who were with me that day.
8. I was given a blessing from a few brothers without asking; they felt inspired to offer me one.
9. I wrote my thoughts periodically in a journal.
10. My heart was filled with love for everyone, my brothers, my family, even those who I knew were not my friends. I was full of love for my Savior and everyone.
11. That morning I looked up into the sky, and toward the horizon. I think I was so disconnected from my physical body (from all the praying and fasting) that it was easier to pierce the veil as I heard the sound of angels singing. I continued to push through the veil when I saw the Lord in the distance upon His Throne. That's when my Baptism of Fire happened.
12. I burst into praise and spoke things of which I have no recollection, because I was so filled with emotion.
13. When it was over I checked with the Lord to see whether I had indeed experienced my Baptism of Fire, and was given an unequivocal YES. I asked whether I now had my Calling and Election and was also told, "Yes."

After having such a powerful experience, I wondered what I was supposed to do next. I continued to pray and study and follow the promptings I had received. Little did I know I was only six months away from having my full encounter with the Lord.

For behold, again I say unto you that if ye will enter

> in by the way, and receive the Holy Ghost, it will show unto you all things what ye should do. Behold, this is the doctrine of Christ, and there will be no more doctrine given until after he shall manifest himself unto you in the flesh. And when he shall manifest himself unto you in the flesh, the things which he shall say unto you shall ye observe to do. (2 Nephi 32:5,6)

At the time I felt that I had such a long way to go. What must I do to come to my Lord and be in His presence? The world seems to be falling apart and the signs of His coming are all around us. I need to come to Him, but how? This was the continual direction of my prayers. I needed to know what the Lord wanted me to do.[151] I soon came to realize He was answering my prayers as fast as I was able and willing to receive the instructions.

---

[151] 2 Nephi 32:3

The Keys to the Door

Chapter Thirteen

I had a vision where I saw a large wooden door with many locks up and down the left face of it. Each lock required a unique key to open it. I had a large ring of keys in my hand and needed to know which to use for each individual lock. It was a delicate and patient process, but one by one I turned and tried the keys until I opened each one of them. Finally, as I opened the last lock I stared at the door. All I had to do was turn the knob and go inside.

The vision of the keys and the locks is an interesting visual metaphor. In the LDS Church, the keys are associated with the Brethren and the Priesthood. I believe it is true that only the President or "prophet" has the full keys of the Church. Indeed, the President of the LDS Church, his administration, the General Presidency, and all to whom the President will grant authority, have the power to administer in the affairs of the Church. In Church ordinances, temple ordinances, and other affairs.

But the Lord has shown me that I can go directly to Him and don't need the permission of any man to knock on the door of heaven. I can worship, pray, ask, and do anything that He commands me to do with a sure knowledge that I am accepted of Him.

I have tried to construct a detailed list of keys that I think made a difference for me in coming to the Lord. I was applying each of these when I pierced the veil and had my Second Comforter experience. I acknowledge that each person's experience may be different than mine, but it's worth noting the process that opened the door for me.

THE KEYS THAT OPEN THE DOOR

1. Desire
2. Be as a Little Child
3. Asking Forgiveness
4. A Great Sacrifice
5. Bathe in Light
6. Praise
7. Take Time to be Holy
8. Gift of Tongues
9. Fasting
10. Seeing with an Eye of Faith

DESIRE

The day before I had my Second Comforter I heard a voice say to me, "Do you truly hunger and thirst after righteousness? Is there anything in your life more important than me?"

“No, Lord” was my answer. I felt ready.

The Sunday before it happened was fairly normal. I went to church and did some home teaching afterwards. I felt a subtle anxiousness knowing that I would be praying and taking time the following morning. It was like I was preparing for an important date or interview. I didn’t exactly know what to expect, but I knew something was coming.

I’ve wondered why some people have great experiences in life and others do not. Why do some people seem to be blessed with more talents than others? I’ve known people that can play the piano or sing like a professional, and some can’t even hum a tune on key. Most of us seem to be capable in some areas, and totally deficient in others.

There are people who seem to be pretty good at a lot of things, but not particularly talented at any one thing. And the challenges of life seem to just come easy for them, and they don’t like to put forth too much effort. I don’t know if it’s because they are perfectionists and become easily discouraged, or just lose interest? Maybe it’s easier to just be comfortable where you are?

I see other people who aren’t particularly talented, but because they are so tenacious and determined they persevere despite their weakness, and, like the tortoise and the hair, they make remarkable progress. Before you know it they are leading the rest of us.

This is the kind of desire that you need to come to the Lord. You have to want it so bad that you are willing to do ANYTHING to make it happen. You can't just hope you'll find God. You can't just desire to see God. You can't just plead for God to open the door. You need to bang on that door, push yourself in, and chase the Lord all the way to the highest realms of the Heavens! The Lord will be smiling and encouraging you the whole way.[152]

When Nephi came to the Lord it was because he wanted to know what his father Lehi knew.[153] He desired to see for himself, and so he asked. His desire was pure. This is the key. You must pray with "real intent, nothing wavering."[154] Make your intentions known to the Lord, and then let the chase begin. Don't settle, don't give up, and please don't listen to those negative thoughts from the Adversary telling you it's hopeless and presumptuous for you to think you're special enough to visit the God of creation. That's stupid talk. You are going to need to fight off those familiar spirits.

BE AS A LITTLE CHILD

---

[152] This is not to be confused with being obnoxious or uninvited. To "push" means to be relentless in your quest to find God. In the section where we discussed "crying unto the Lord" I wrote about the parable of the persistent widow who cried unto the judge night and day until she received what she wanted. This is the mind set of those who will find the Lord. (Luke 18:1-8)

[153] 1 Nephi 11:1

[154] James 1:6

As I looked back on my experience, I realized that this was an important factor in coming to the Lord. How does becoming as a little child help one to have their Second Comforter?

Children have a much different outlook on the world. Little children are curious, believing, trusting, and open to new ideas. When we grow up and become adults we tend to see the world in terms of absolutes rather than "what ifs," and we set up walls of unbelief. When I was a little boy I dreamed of being a cowboy until somebody told me it was impossible. Why can't I be a cowboy? Why can't I learn to rope and shoot and wear a big white hat? Now I ask a bigger question—why can't I have my Second Comforter?

> At the same time came the disciples unto Jesus, saying, Who is the greatest in the kingdom of heaven? And Jesus called a little child unto him, and set him in the midst of them, And said, Verily I say unto you, Except ye be converted, and become as little children, ye shall not enter into the kingdom of heaven. Whosoever therefore shall humble himself as this little child, the same is greatest in the kingdom of heaven. And whoso shall receive one such little child in my name receiveth me. (Matthew 18:1-5)

The quality that the Lord mentions here specifically is humility. To be humble is to be teachable. Other synonyms of teachable are: impressionable, lowly[155], malleable, moldable, receptive, thirsty for knowledge,[156] trainable, unpretentious, and willing.[157] Can you see how this would qualify one to be great in the Lord's kingdom? Are these attributes that describe yourself?

The opposite of teachable is stubborn, obstinate, headstrong, inflexible, uncompromising, stiff-necked,[158] and resistant. These are also attributes of pride, and that is something few children possess.

I realized that when I learned to lean on the Lord more, and not accept the world's view on things, I began to grow closer to the Lord. Alma talked about having faith like a seed,[159] (Christ compared it to a mustard seed[160]) and that by this all things are possible to him that believes. Does a child trust their parent to catch them when they jump? We must trust the Lord implicitly if we wish to come to Him. We must be willing to let go of inhibitions and vanity. We have to get used to the idea that we are going to be seen as peculiar to everyone who is unfamiliar with the Spirit and the realms of Heaven.

Another interesting quality of a child is their inclination to

---

155 Matthew 11:29
156 Matthew 5:6
157 D&C 64:34
158 Jarom 1:4
159 Alma 32:28
160 Matthew 17:20

ask questions, lots of questions. When my kids want something, they knock until I answer the door. They call on the phone over and over again if they can't reach me. Boy, that can drive me crazy, but I love them and usually give them what they need if it's for their good.

> And I say unto you, Ask, and it shall be given you; seek, and ye shall find; knock, and it shall be opened unto you. For every one that asketh receiveth; and he that seeketh findeth; and to him that knocketh it shall be opened. If a son shall ask bread of any of you that is a father, will he give him a stone? or if *he ask* a fish, will he for a fish give him a serpent? Or if he shall ask an egg, will he offer him a scorpion? If ye then, being evil, know how to give good gifts unto your children: how much more shall *your* heavenly Father give the Holy Spirit to them that ask him? (Luke 11:9-13)

Think about what you want to ask the Lord. Make a list if you think it will help you sort out your questions and remember. I had been asking to come to Him for many years before it finally occurred. I don't think it was only asking that made the difference; it was taking action when he gave me a bread crumb. It's like the Lord gave me my chores and I just did it, whatever it was. Be like a child and you will find Him.

ASKING FORGIVENESS

This is a tricky subject for some of us because we may wonder whether forgiveness requires us to do much on our own, or is Jesus' Atonement all that is required? Must we simply ask God for forgiveness? What should we ask forgiveness for? How can we know what needs to be forgiven by the Lord and what is our responsibility in this process? If you find yourself in this quandary, the solution is easy: you ask Him.

In the "Four Steps to Powerful Prayer,"[161] step 1 is "Being clean unto the Lord." How do you deal with someone you've wronged? You may need to go and talk with them. But what if they did something to harm you? You need to forgive them also. Sometimes that is the hardest thing to do. Remember, it's much more effective if you forgive them, or ask forgiveness in person.

I know this may be unsettling news for some of us, but we need to have a clear conscience before the Lord. I remember my wife had an experience when she called up an old employer she had bad feelings about and apologized for not being a better employee. He couldn't even remember who she was. This man who was unkind to her was now a Bishop, and they had a sweet conversation of reconciliation.

---

[161] Pg. 39 of this book.

After you knock off all on the list of "please forgive me," then focus on a particular sin or sins that may prevent you from coming to the Lord. What might those be? When you ask the Lord, He will surely bring them to your remembrance.

Some of us may be inhibited by Babylon or even addictions of the flesh. It could be as simple as too much football or gummy worms. What is the focus of your idle time? What are your idols? When the Lord said, "Thou shalt not covet," what was he talking about? Anything that takes precedence and priority over Him is idolatry. This is a sin, and requires repentance in sackcloth and ashes. He wants your heart and soul, for you to love Him with all your might, mind and strength. This is what it means to repent. Overcoming the power or weight of sin and addiction is foolhardy without turning our hearts completely over to the Lord. Just ask anyone dealing with the sin of alcoholism or even pornography. Without God, what can you hope to achieve?

And then comes perhaps the most difficult part—y**ou must forgive yourself**.

Every one of us has a secret life; sins that we are ashamed to admit. Satan will throw it in your face every day. "You are a vile sinner and have no place thinking you could ever have your Second Comforter experience!" Does that sound familiar? Don't believe him. DO NOT BELIEVE IT FOR A SECOND. It is a lie.

Remember the parable of the prodigal son? The son squandered his inheritance and was eating with the pigs; when he thought perhaps his father would allow him to at least be a servant, he decided to come home reluctantly, expecting very little. But when his Father saw him from a distance he did not wait. He ran out to meet him, and hugged him close and kissed him. He put shoes on his feet, placed a robe upon him, put a ring on his finger, and made a great feast for all to come and welcome back his son; his son who once was lost, now was found.[162] This may be you, and it certainly is me.

Don't let anything stop you from coming home to Him.

A GREAT SACRIFICE

One thing I've learned from others who have experienced their Second Comforter is that they were tested to see if they would sacrifice all things. What is the thing that would be hardest for you to lay upon the altar as a sacrifice for God?[163]

I think of Abraham being asked to sacrifice his only son.[164] Can you imagine his pain? Jonah couldn't bear to go to those unrepentant people of Nineveh,[165] but he came

---

[162] Luke 15:11-32
[163] Matthew 19:16-24
[164] Genesis 22:1-13
[165] Jonah 3

around to it. Some have sacrificed their very lives![166] Each of us have challenges and trouble in our life. The question is how you handle them and whether you consecrate them to the Lord.

When money is tight and you can't make ends meet, do you tell the Lord you love him no matter what? When someone you love dies needlessly and regretfully, how do you approach God? When you feel your hopes are dashed, do you blame God, or ask Him what He wants you to learn from all this?

I have reflected on the many difficult experiences of my life and have seen a pattern. I'm not perfect, I've whined and kicked, and complained, but I came around and eventually saw that the Lord was always with me.

The last sacrifice, that tilted the scale in my favor toward opening the heavens started about a year ago. The Lord revealed to my wife and I that we were to change the way we paid our tithing; which isn't the kind of thing you would do lightly. I have been a full tithe payer my entire life, even in my most difficult days financially, I always gave one-tenth

---

[166] ". . . When a man has offered in sacrifice all that he has, for the truth's sake, not even withholding his life, and believing before God that he has been called to make this sacrifice, because he seeks to do his will, he does know most assuredly, that God does and will accept his sacrifice & offering, & that he has not nor will not seek his face in vain. . ." Lectures on Faith 6:7

to the Church. What is the Lord asking me to do? Why would He have me do something contrary to a church commandment? Again, He said, "Relax, and trust me."

I was told by the Lord that we would continue to pay our tithing, but in a different manner than before. We were instructed to put our tithing in a separate account, instead of submitting it to the Bishop. From here, we would give these sacred funds to individuals and families, as the Lord would instruct us by the Spirit. Each time this occurred, we were to keep a record in a tithing journal of the amount and what transpired and who was blessed. This has since become a source of rich blessings for my wife and I as we were able to actively seek out those who we could be instruments in the Lord's hands to help. We would pray about specific amounts and specific people. Usually, they were complete strangers. What a joyful experience this has been, but sure enough the pied piper came calling–tithing settlement.

My wife and I dreaded having to tell our Bishop. We love our ward and the Bishop is a great man. What would he think? He came by our house and he brought with him the receipts. I had to explain what was happening. I said that the Lord had instructed us to do it this way. He reminded me that as our Bishop we could not have a temple recommend without paying tithing. Before he left he hugged me with the affection of a loving parent. I felt sad that the Bishop was in this awkward position, and I wondered how this would all play out.

Two weeks later my wife and I met in his office. The Bishop said that he told the Stake President what we had said and that the Stake President had a message for us: "You are getting your inspiration from the wrong source." We handed over our temple recommends and waited to hear what the Bishop would say. He looked at us and asked, "If President Monson was here right now and told you to pay your tithing, what would you say?"

I responded, "Bishop, if the Lord was here and said to pay it His way and President Monson another, what would you do?" He grimaced at my reply. The Bishop was kind and we left wondering how this would affect things in the future. With family temple weddings around the corner, this would surely create strain on the family.

Joseph Smith said, "But we cannot keep all the commandments without first knowing them, and we cannot expect to know all, or more than we now know unless we comply with or keep those we have already received. **That which is wrong under one circumstance, may be, and often is, right under another**." [167]

Was this the final sacrifice I had to make to part the veil? I chose to listen to the Lord's voice and chose Him over the advice of my Bishop, the Stake President, and the entire LDS

---

[167] Latter-Day Saints Millennial Star, Vol. 19, History of Joseph Smith, Aug. 1842, pg. 774

Church's requirements to enter the House of the Lord.[168] No, it wasn't as hard as Abraham's sacrifice, but it was still heart wrenching.

> For a man to lay down his all, his character and reputation, his honor and applause, his good name among men, his houses, his lands, his brothers and sisters, his wife and children, and even his own life also, counting all things but filth and dross for the excellency of the knowledge of Jesus Christ, requires more than mere belief or supposition that he is doing the will of God, but actual knowledge; realizing that when these sufferings are ended he will enter into eternal rest, and be a partaker of the glory of God. (Lectures on Faith 6:5)

I trusted in the witness I received from the Lord that we were doing the right thing. Two weeks later I had my Second Comforter experience.

BATHE IN THE LIGHT

This is something unique that the Lord started to teach me about three months before my Second Comforter experience. I had never read about this or heard of anything like this before, but I feel it made a difference.

---

[168] I am not suggesting you change the way you personally pay your tithing. This was the sacrifice we were asked to do. Your sacrifice will likely be different.

It began with the Lord telling me, by His Spirit, after having received the Baptism of Fire, to imagine seeing light coming from my body. I would close my eyes and imagine a white aura around my hand. I would do this until I sensed it and could see it. From there I would try and see an aura around my entire body. Sometimes I would stand in the bathroom and relax my eyes and then imagine having this light around me.

This little exercise of my mind began to be a ritual for how I prepared my thoughts. Whenever I would kneel or sit to pray, I would take a moment to see if I could extend my light. I got to the point where I would try and fill the room with the light from my spirit, which would connect to me from the glory of God. It was like God's glory was the power source and I was the light bulb.

I would ask the Lord to help me. I could hear Him in my mind encouraging me to push it more. "Brighter, brighter, as bright as the sun!"[169] would come the thoughts in my mind.[170] I could eventually feel the light, as if it were a tangible pulse around me. Expanding the light was a type of exercise. I still don't fully understand its significance, but I believe it prepared my mind and heart to make me clean in order to come to the Lord.

Toward the end, before I had my first experience, I even felt the light flowing down over me like water. I actually began

---

[169] Joseph Smith–History 1:16

[170] Alma 19:6

to bathe in the light.[171] I would ask the Lord to heal me, cleanse me, and make me holy to my very essence. This was not just fluorescent, artificial light; this was the very glory of God washing over my Spirit! This was a very real experience for me and I believe it was a critical key in opening the door.

PRAISE

The Second Step of the "Pray with Power" is to express gratitude to the Lord. To be more specific, we praise Him. I don't think I truly understood the power of praise until just recently. Why would God want us to praise Him? Does He need our flattery and compliments to keep the Kingdom afloat? Of course not.

I heard a friend once explain that it was like going to a concert. The audience feeds off the energy of the performers and people reciprocate their appreciation by singing along and raising their hands. In return the performer plays harder and tunes in to the audience and together they have a great concert and experience. This is a simplistic analogy, but God wants to bless us. When we have our hearts in tune with Him, great power ensues.

How does one praise with power? A nice "thank you" is a good start. I've tried many different prayers of praise. You can begin by thanking the Lord for all your blessings. You can thank Him for all the hard stuff too. Did you ever think

---

[171] D&C 88:6-13

to praise Him when life is at its worst? That's powerful! That's what Nephi did while he was bound tightly to the mast of the boat for four days.[172] That's praise!

King David was a master of praise.[173] He wrote The Book of Psalms in the Old Testament. It's all about praise for God. Praise is one of the most powerful tools you have to open the windows of Heaven. The Israelites were obsessed with it; they would praise God in everything they did: instrumental music, song, dance, coloring, architecture, how they wore clothes, everything. And its purpose was to bless them.

> And it came to pass, when the priests were come out of the holy *place:* (for all the priests *that were* present were sanctified, *and* did not *then* wait by course:
>
> Also the Levites *which were* the singers, all of them of Asaph, of Heman, of Jeduthun, with their sons and their brethren, *being* arrayed in white linen, having cymbals and psalteries and harps, stood at the east end of the altar, and with them an hundred and twenty priests sounding with trumpets:)
>
> It came even to pass, as the trumpeters and singers *were* as one, to make one sound to be heard in

---

[172] 1 Nephi 18:11-16

[173] 1 Chronicles 13:8

> praising and thanking the Lord; and when they lifted up *their* voice with the trumpets and cymbals and instruments of musick, and praised the Lord, *saying,* For *he is* good; for his mercy *endureth* for ever: that *then* the house was filled with a cloud, *even* the house of the Lord; So that the priests could not stand to minister by reason of the cloud: for the glory of the Lord had filled the house of God. (2 Chronicles 5:11-14)

The power of these Israelites praising literally brought down the glory of the Lord to the extent they had difficulty standing in the holy place!

How can you praise God? The more creative the better. I wrote my own "prayer of praise," which I included at the end of this book. You should consider writing the Lord a letter from your heart and reading it to Him.

Hymns and poetry are a great way to praise.[174] I have my favorite hymns and songs, but I like to sometimes use my own words and make up lyrics as I sing to the Lord. Spending a portion of your prayers praising in this manner cracks the doors to heaven wide open. As you get good at praise, it will lead you to the inevitable—the Gift of Tongues. We'll be talking about this in a few pages.

---

[174] Psalms 69:30, Psalms 95:1-2, Colossians 3:16

Praise the Lord with ALL YOUR HEART,[175] and feel the glory of His kingdom begin to fill you from head to toe. This is powerful information, and a little outside the comfort zone of most LDS people. I know it sounds unconventional, but you will need to throw out many traditional, and formal restraints before this is all through.

When was the last time you saw a member stand up in Sacrament meeting and shout, "Hallelujah!"[176] Why not? It certainly is not a part of our culture, and so people would think you were crazy if you did. Remember when we were little tykes in our primary meetings and we were taught that acceptable reverence to the Lord was a bowed head, hands clasped or arms folded, quiet in our chairs listening attentively to the speaker, and raising our hands when called upon? These customs are more about respect than reverence. One cannot have praise without respect, but we can have respect without reverence. Reverence is the attitude of the heart.

Praise is pure exuberant joy for the Lord and it doesn't require whispering. True reverence is honoring what is sacred and knowing what is not. Do not confuse the two. The purpose of this section is not to say you need to get loud and rowdy at church. It is to say that an attitude of praise requires you to open yourself to expression. Give

---

[175] Ephesians 5:19

[176] Psalms 135:3

great attention to how you praise and you will have success in coming to Him.

TAKE TIME TO BE HOLY

If you want anything good in this life it will require a sacrifice of your time. You have 24 hours in a day; how will you choose to divide that up? What are your priorities? The things in which we choose to focus our energy and thoughts upon usually become our obsessions, and thereby we see results over time. Can the average person become a great musician without practice? Is it possible to have a healthy body without exercise and hard work? You will not have the faith necessary to come to the Lord unless you are willing to allocate times of your day and week to be holy for Him.

Our dreams and desires usually lead us to action. What is important to you? Where is your treasure?

> Lay not up for yourselves treasures upon earth, where moth and rust doth corrupt, and where thieves break through and steal: But lay up for yourselves treasures in heaven, where neither moth nor rust doth corrupt, and where thieves do not break through nor steal: For where your treasure is, there will your heart be also. (Matthew 6:19-21)

I have found that the key is to not just do things randomly during the day (although that's not bad), but to **purposefully** take time to be holy. I like to set aside an hour or two if possible to approach the Lord. When you set aside this kind of time, you are demonstrating that you are serious about your relationship with Him and results will happen.

It takes a little planning to make the time effective. This is "holy time," meaning that it is special, and anything you designate as special to the Lord will have His approval if it is approached by the Spirit and according to His will.

> But behold, I say unto you that ye must pray always, and not faint; that ye must not perform any thing unto the Lord save in the first place ye shall pray unto the Father in the name of Christ, that he will consecrate thy performance unto thee, that thy performance may be for the welfare of thy soul. (2 Nephi 32:9)

Here are some of the things we can do to consecrate our time unto the Lord:

1. Pray and worship.
2. Study the scriptures.
3. Serve others.
4. Take the Sacrament.
5. Write in a journal about sacred experiences.
6. Spend time with friends and family in spiritual and sacred conversation.

7. Sing hymns to the Lord.
8. Write poetry or spend time in other artistic activities dedicated to praise.
9. Keep the Sabbath Day Holy.
10. Observe the sacred Holy Days of the Old Testament.
11. Visit the temple of the Lord.
12. Serve in missionary efforts under the Lord's direction.
13. Perform any kind of unconventional task or activity as directed by the Lord.

Most good people don't spend more than a few minutes a day praying. Most people don't pray at all, but you must have a deep relationship with the Lord if you desire to come to Him. I would refer to the chapter in this book on "Pray with Power" and master those concepts. I would suggest planning your prayer time and having a strategy for how you will approach the Lord to make this time even more "holy." Like anything else, you will get out of it what you put into it.

Joseph Smith would plan a special time each day to go to the Lord in prayer. "I have visited a grove which is just back of the town almost every day, where I can be secluded from the eyes of any mortal and there give vent to all the feeling of my heart in meditation and prayer."[177]

---

[177] Joseph Smith to Emma Smith, June 6, 1832, Greenville, Indiana, manuscript at the Chicago Historical Society

Many prophets in the Book of Mormon tell of setting aside special time to seek the Lord: Lehi,[178] Nephi,[179] Enos,[180] and Alma[181] to name a few. If you make this the most important time of your day, you will become holy to the Lord and your desire to do His will increases and you will become a powerful instrument in His hands.

THE SACRAMENT

I have been taking the Sacrament ever since I was old enough to reach out and grab that little cup and piece of bread, and yet I'm barely beginning to understand the significance of this act. The time we spend taking the Sacrament is one of the most holy things we can do before we approach the Lord. It expresses our desire to make a covenant with Him and not only makes the time holy, but us as well. That is one of the beauties of sacrificing our time for the Lord—we become holy in the process.

When the Savior gathered his apostles together and offered them the bread and wine, he was doing something special that He wanted them to remember.

> And as they were eating, Jesus took bread, and blessed it, and brake it, and gave it to the disciples, and said, Take, eat; this is my body. And he took

---

[178] 1 Nephi 1:5

[179] 1 Nephi 18:3

[180] Enos 1:3,4

[181] Alma 17:3

> the cup, and gave thanks, and gave it to them, saying, Drink ye all of it; for this is my blood of the new testament, which is shed for many for the remission of sins. (Matthew 26:26-28)

In the Sacrament prayers recorded in Moroni 4 and 5 we get the wording the Lord would have us use, as translated into English. For me, this is more than a renewal of our baptismal covenant; it's a promise that we will receive the Lord fully by covenant; that we will not just keep His commandments, but that we will also take His name upon us. What does that mean? Does it imply we will think of Him sometimes and be good people? It means a lot more than that. He is promising that we can be born again, quickened in the Spirit, made new in the blood of the Lamb, and have His name burned into our souls; thereby we receive the Gift of the Holy Ghost and the Baptism of Fire, and will always have His Spirit to be with us!

We are literally remembering His blood covenant. In ancient Israel when a covenant was made an animal would be cut in half, right down the middle. Standing on the bloody ground, two people would make an oath to each other. This is called "cutting the covenant."[182] Then the two oath makers would walk between the sacrifice and pledge themselves to each other in covenant.[183] Then they would say that if they didn't keep this covenant, may they be cut asunder as these animals. (This gives the temple cuttings a

---

[182] Genesis 15:7-21

[183] Jeremiah 34:18-20

whole new meaning.)

As a permanent sign of their covenant, they would take a knife and make a small cut in the palm of their hand. Then they would clasp hands, allowing the blood to intermingle as they symbolically became one with each other. As the wound would heal, the scar, or mark, would be like a wedding ring to stand as a symbol of the covenant between the two people. When they would meet they would hold up their hands as a reminder of the covenant made between them.[184] Jesus has a permanent mark on his hands and has stood on bloody ground for us.

The ancient covenant ceremony often ended with a meal of bread and wine. As the two covenant makers sat together, they would share the bread and wine and say, "I give myself to you, as a sign of our covenant."[185] Thereby the covenant relationship was emphasized, and they would never forget. Jesus made the ultimate eternal covenant for us, and we are reminded of this every time we take His holy Sacrament!

In my preparations for coming to Him, I was told to take the Sacrament each time, every morning, as I prepared to part the veil. I personalized the words as such:

> O God, the Eternal Father, I ask thee in the name of thy Son, Jesus Christ, to bless and sanctify this

---

[184] 1 Samuel 20:16, Ezekiel 17:18, Job 17:3

[185] Genesis 31:51-54, Exodus 24:3-11, Leviticus 7:11-16

> bread to my soul as I partake of it; that I may eat in remembrance of the body of thy Son, and witness unto thee, O God, the Eternal Father, that I am willing to take upon me the name of thy Son, and always remember him, and keep his commandments which he hath given me, that I may always have his Spirit to be with me. Amen. (Moroni 4:3)
>
> O God, the Eternal Father, I ask thee, in the name of thy Son, Jesus Christ, to bless and sanctify this wine to my soul as I drink of it, that I may do it in remembrance of the blood of thy Son, which was shed for me; that I may witness unto thee, O God, the Eternal Father, that I do always remember him, that I may have his Spirit to be with me. Amen. (Moroni 5:2)

Yes, I had permission from the Lord to do this.

Make your Sacrament experience holy and you will be holy to the Lord.

THE SABBATH

A little earlier I mentioned that after I experienced my Baptism of Fire I wondered what the Lord expected me to do next. I received some revelation regarding the Sabbath, and the Lord told me to prepare myself.

Each person must decide which seventh day they

> wish to honor as the Sabbath. Its purpose is to point one's heart to God, to praise Him, to learn of Him. The calendar used was originally based upon the new moon, because it was the only way to mark the days. Today you can choose as you will, but if you choose to do the lunar calendar you must decide how you plan to use the extra days. Originally, the days were longer and the Sabbath was longer (before the flood). Now you have extra days throughout the year. If you choose to use the lunar, include the new moon days as holy days. This is more than normally required, but will allow you to follow the pattern. The act of turning from the pagan calendar to God's signs in the Heavens is a great act of honor and I, **God, will also honor you for such an act**. But again, it is left unto thee to make this decision. My servant Joseph was told that it was left unto him to decide when he asked the same question. Use wisdom and know that how the Sabbath affects your heart and desires is what is important. You are loved. (Personal Revelation 6/30/2015)

The Lord told me again on 11/22/2015 that this is important for me:

> I asked, "Lord, what am I to do in regard to the Sabbath?"
>
> "You shall be taught more perfectly of my ways in relation to the times and seasons. The Holy Days

> and convocations. All things must be done in order, for I am not the author of confusion. Follow me and your path shall be made clear."

In January of 2016 my wife and I decided together to begin adhering to the lunar Sabbath in addition to our regular Sunday worship. The Sabbath Day is one of the most important specific things the Lord has commanded we do in taking time to be holy.[186]

This is how my wife and I decided to structure our Sabbath:

It should be a joyful time with the family (not solemn, but also not loud laughter either). We will try to make it a time of the week that the kids will actually look forward to. All of us will work together, if possible, to have the food and the house prepared beforehand. Then we will set a time in the evening around sunset, when everyone will be there, to gather together and start the ceremony.

This is our Sabbath plan:

1. My wife or I will light what we call our Sabbath Candles (one for each member of the family) and offer a prayer for each family member. This occurs on the eve of the Sabbath. (The Sabbath goes from sunset to sunset.)
2. Sing joyful songs.
3. Sacrament Blessing.
4. Dinner.

---

[186] Exodus 20:8

5. Conversation.
6. Morning Study.
7. Spend the day doing special (holy) activities dedicated to God, family, and service. (Plan something special with the family.) Avoid mindless internet, movies, regular work, and cleaning.
8. End the Sabbath with a family prayer asking for the Lord's protection.

Here is how we decided to follow the lunar Sabbath:[187]

- I will mark the new moon[188] for each month and from here count the 8th, 15th, 22nd, and 29th day to know the Sabbath.
- I will celebrate the New Moons by making them holy, a day of fasting.
- I can use the available websites and check the moon phases to know when the Sabbath occurs. http://www.moonconnection.com/moon_phases_calendar.phtml
- I will have a calendar marked with all holy days and Sabbaths as a record.

---

[187] For more scripture and insights regarding Lunar Sabbath I recommend creationcalendar.com

[188] The New Moon is the night when the moon's lighter half is facing the sun, giving the side we see a dark silhouette. Counting seven additional days begins the first Sabbath of the lunar month.

I know this is a hard adjustment for many people, especially if your working time is not flexible; you will need to pray for your own revelation for how you should proceed. I'm simply including this because it was another sacrifice I did just before I had my experience with the Lord. At the time I received my Second Comforter I had been living the original Sabbath observance with my family for two weeks. Is it any coincidence that the Lord came to me shortly thereafter?

Making yourself holy by "taking time to be holy," may be one of the single most important principles to coming into the presence of the Lord. The ancient Hebrews were taught many sacred rites and rituals to keep them holy and focused upon the Lord, but as it says in the Book of Mormon, "They looked beyond the mark."[189] The purpose of all this is not the act itself, but the positioning of our hearts toward Jesus Christ. When you become holy you will have no problem approaching the Lord.

GIFT OF TONGUES

This particular gift of the spirit has always been a kind of anomaly, a mystic conundrum, that eluded my understanding. Will the Lord simply cause me to speak an unknown foreign language out of the clear blue sky?

I served a mission in an area where I had to learn a foreign language, which was difficult. I learned it faster than most

---

[189] Jacob 4:14

people; but was that the gift of tongues? The Lord did bless me, but for some reason this miracle of the gift of tongues seemed to be something different altogether.

I began to seriously study what it was about. By my own experience, I had witnessed every gift listed by Moroni in his farewell address,[190] except the gift of tongues. We are told to seek after the best gifts. This is one of the last he listed; was I to seek this gift? The answer I was given was—yes!

Did you know that in the early days of the Church, the Gift of Tongues was a basic and fundamental part of their worship?

At the dedication services for the Kirtland Temple David Whitmer bore testimony that he saw three angels at the Temple that day, "passing up the south aisle, and there came a shock on the house like the sound of a mighty rushing wind, and almost every man in the house arose, and **hundreds of them were speaking in tongues, prophesying or declaring visions, almost with one voice**" [191]

> Joseph Smith stated, "All the congregation simultaneously arose, being moved upon by an invisible power; **many began to speak in tongues and prophesy; others saw glorious visions; and I beheld the Temple was filled with angels, which fact I declared to the congregation**. The people of

---

[190] Moroni 10:15,16

[191] Journal of Discourses, 11:10

the neighborhood came running together (hearing an unusual sound within, and seeing a bright light like a pillar of fire resting upon the Temple), and were astonished at what was taking place" [192]

The Prophet Joseph on another occasion stated, "...The gifts which follow them that believe and obey the gospel...began to be poured out among us, as in ancient days; for as we...elders were assembled in conference on the twenty-second day of January [1833] I spoke to the conference in another tongue and was followed in the same gift by Brother Zebedee Coltrin, and he by Brother William Smith, after which the Lord poured out his Spirit in a miraculous manner **until all the elders spoke in tongues, and several members, both male and female**. Great and glorious were the divine manifestations of the Holy Spirit. **Praises were sung to God and the Lamb; speaking and praying, all in tongues, occupied the conference, until a late hour at night,** so rejoiced were we at the return of these long absent blessings. On the twenty-third, we again assembled in conference; when, **after much speaking, singing, praying and praising God, all in tongues, we proceeded to the washing of feet**..." [193]

---

[192] History of the Church, 2:428

[193] (HC 1:277-78).

If they could do it then, then why not now? Is this not another wall of unbelief that has crept in among our traditions? I was determined to try and obtain this gift, do or die.

The first experience I had with the gift of tongues was October of 2015. It was early in the morning and I was on my knees asking the Lord what, or how, I was to do this? I began to praise God with all my heart, expressing my love and gratitude. I heard a voice in my head say, "Just relax and speak the sounds that feel good." I started to say what sounded like strange syllables and it felt awkward and foolish, but I kept going. Within a few seconds, what was strange began to cause my heart to fill with love and the Spirit poured out upon me in great measure. It was a pure form of praise that I had not felt since I had my Baptism of Fire a few months earlier. I only spoke in tongues for less than 30 seconds, but it had a profound impact on my desires to get closer to God and do it again.

I decided that every time I would say my private prayers I would try and speak in tongues. It was my personal prayer and praise language. I felt like a foreigner trying to express my love through sound. I didn't care what I sounded like, although I tried to feel like I was saying something. Sometimes I wondered if the Spirit was guiding me in my words.

Before long I noticed that while saying prayers or giving blessings I would hear clear words come to my mind in a language I did not know. The words or phrases came so forcefully I felt compelled to speak them. I would pray and ask the Lord what it meant and would be given the meaning. Always, the spirit would strongly confirm the validity of the experience.

I learned by faith and prayer that there really was something happening when the Gift of Tongues was used.

FASTING

This was curiously the last thing the Lord had me study before my Second Comforter. I had fasted many times and studied the law of fasting, but I did not fully understand its significance. We are taught in the church to fast from food and water for 24 hours, and while doing so, if we pray earnestly, the Lord will bless us. He will answer our prayers and we will feel His Spirit more abundantly. Yes, this is true.

What I have learned is that part of the process of coming to the Lord is that we need to untether our physical bodies from our spirit as much as possible; thereby our spirit becomes the most sensitive.[194] When King Benjamin said that the natural man was an enemy to God,[195] he was making a powerful statement.

---

[194] D&C 101:37-38

[195] Mosiah 3:19

Have you ever been on a prescription drug that affected your vision and made it difficult to either focus or see clearly? Has your body ever been so tired that your vision blurred and your mind couldn't focus or concentrate? These symptoms are the effect the body has on the spirit as we try to see through the veil. Our physical bodies *are* the veil. Unless we are physically dead and completely untethered to our bodies, or we are able to greatly overcome the flesh by means of fasting, we are going to struggle to have a pure experience. It takes great focus to converse with the Lord.

Moroni 7 has an interesting verse in relation to the importance of our state of mind:

> And because he hath done this, my beloved brethren, have miracles ceased? Behold I say unto you, Nay; neither have angels ceased to minister unto the children of men. For behold, they are subject unto him, to minister according to the word of his command, **showing themselves unto them of strong faith and a firm mind in every form of godliness.** (vs. 29-30)

What is meant by a "firm mind in every form of godliness?" I believe that there are two parts to this statement. First, our minds must be clean of any distractions, impure images, or unworthy thoughts. Second, we must be able to push through the veil by having a firm mind that that does not allow the body to dictate our desires. You must choose the spirit over the body, the mind and will over the desires of the flesh.

Fasting can include more than food and water. All desires of the flesh qualify for "fasting" as we choose the Lord over the natural man. We can choose to fast from TV, movies, sleep, internet, regular work, or anything that shows the Lord that we desire nothing more than to be in His presence.

I plan to work up to longer fasts and see what I can do in the future. The main thing about fasting is that I am saying to the Lord, "I choose you over my body and comfort." When you completely choose to hunger and thirst for righteousness—to come to our Lord and nothing else–then you are ready.

SEEING WITH AN EYE OF FAITH

This is the last principle key that I wanted to share with you before you part the veil and come to the Lord. What should you expect? What is it like to see in the Spirit? I always wondered what it would be like to stand in the presence of the Lord. Would He just walk right up to me in my bedroom? I suppose He could do that, but it doesn't seem to be the standard norm for such things.

Where was Joseph Smith when the Lord came to him? Was he in the grove of trees a short distance from his log home, or somewhere else in the spirit?[196] "All things whatsoever God has seen proper to reveal to us while we are dwelling

[196] Joseph Smith History 1:20

in mortality are revealed to us in the abstract & independent of affinity of this mortal tabernacle—but they are revealed as though we had no bodies at all." (Words of Joseph Smith pg. 360)

Where was Moses when he spoke with the Lord? Was he standing in front of the burning bush, or somewhere else?

> But now mine own eyes have beheld God; but not my natural, but my spiritual eyes, for my natural eyes could not have beheld; for I should have withered and died in his presence; but his glory was upon me; and I beheld his face, for I was transfigured before him. (Moses 1:11)

What about Nephi, Lehi, Isaiah, Abraham, Alma, Moroni, the Brother of Jared? Each is different, but in each instance the Lord seems to have them transfigured and taken to Him in the Spirit.[197]

> And whether they were in the body or out of the body, they could not tell; for it did seem unto them like a transfiguration of them, that they were changed from this body of flesh into an immortal state, that they could behold the things of God. (3 Nephi 28:15)

The prophet Joseph Smith explained that God "dwells in eternal fire; flesh and blood cannot go there, for all

---

[197] D&C 67:10-12

corruption is devoured by the fire. Our God is a consuming fire." [198]

The Apostle Paul noticed something different about his experience:

> It is not expedient for me doubtless to glory. I will come to visions and revelations of the Lord. I knew a man in Christ above fourteen years ago, **whether in the body, I cannot tell; or whether out of the body, I cannot tell:** God knoweth; such an one caught up to the third heaven. [The Third Heaven is the Throne of God.] And I knew such a man, **whether in the body, or out of the body, I cannot tell: God knoweth;** How that he was caught up into paradise, and heard unspeakable words, which it is not lawful for a man to utter. Of such an one will I glory: yet of myself I will not glory, but in mine infirmities. (2 Corinthians 12:1-5)

When I had my Second Comforter experience, my spirit ascended to him. What does this mean? It means that unless Jesus condescends and comes down to earth in the flesh, we must go to him in the spirit. [199]

What does it mean to see in the spirit with an eye of faith? Our spiritual eyes function much differently from our

---

[198] TPJS, p. 367

[199] 3 Nephi 15:23

physical eyes. I don't understand all the science of this, but here is some detail I have learned that is truly remarkable.

> The human eye is far more sophisticated than any camera of a comparable size. The cells on the outer layer of the retina can absorb a single particle of light, or photon, and amplify its energy at least a million times, before transferring it in the form of a nervous signal to the back of the brain. The iris, which functions as the eye's diaphragm, is automatically controlled. The cornea has just the right curvature. The lens is focused by miniature muscles, which are also controlled automatically by feedback. The final result of this visual system, still imperfectly understood in its entirety, is a clear, colored, and three-dimensional image inside the brain that we perceive as external. We never see reality, but only an internal representation of it that our brain constructs for us continually. (The Cosmic Serpent, by Jeremy Darby, pg. 104)

So what is truly real and tangible? Is it what we see with our physical eyes, or our spiritual? Because we have trouble seeing spiritually, does that make it less real?

Scientists have studied the human brain and found that when we dream or have visions, the central part of our brain, the pineal gland, is activated to a certain degree. This has anciently been known as the "third eye." This is not particularly important, except to understand that there is a reality to seeing in the spirit. It is just as real and sensory as our physical eyes, but less understood.

When you see in the spirit it will not be the same experience as seeing in the flesh. People often describe a heightened sense of awareness. One can see in all directions as they choose. You can see up close or panoramic. You can see through, around, up, down, or all around. Colors can be more pronounced, or indescribable. But this is how it is for those who are focused and experienced with seeing in the spirit. Perhaps for a new visionary, you will be like the newborn infant in his mother's arms, struggling to focus and see. Your first experience seeing in the spirit may be difficult.

I called this section "Seeing with an Eye of Faith," and this may be the section of the book where people stumble the most in their understanding. If your perceptions of how you will receive the Second Comforter do not match your expectations, you may choose to disconnect and never come to the Lord. This is where the "wall of unbelief" can be a curse. What do I mean by that? Everything about our faith is based on prior beliefs and our willingness to learn or relearn what we think we know. There is much in this book which may already fly in the face of everything you firmly believed was true. Perhaps I have said or will say something foreign to your understanding. Does this mean what I have written is false? Perhaps you should consider the words the Lord told me: "Relax. You will know what I say is true, simply by asking and receiving your own revelation. You can know for yourself!"

When you begin to crack open the door and see with an eye of faith, expect things to blur and then focus. Expect to see glimpses, followed by blackouts or disappearing images. Keep focusing and talking with the Lord. Don't phase out because you think it's your imagination. Trust yourself, trust the Lord, and push forward. Keep chasing the Lord, all the way to the courts of Heaven. Don't give up, don't get negative. Hold on to the images you see and keep revisiting them until they expand and lead to another. At first you will feel like a person trying to focus who hasn't slept for days. You are tethered to the flesh, and until you completely let go and focus on the Lord and what he is showing you, it will seem a little disconnected. Remember the Savior's words, "Peace, be still."

Sometimes you must simply let your ability to "see with an eye of faith" grow within you like a new talent, ability, or even a "seed." Do you remember Alma's allegory of the seed growing into a tree and eventually bearing fruit? You must nourish the seed and if it grows you know it is a good seed. If it dies it may be that it wasn't on good ground or wasn't nourished properly. Your seed of faith is your imagination. Here we have one of the biggest walls of unbelief that many deal with. "Imagination" is a dirty word to those who are scientific, or critics of all things spiritual. These are people who seek for a sign. "How can I know this is not a trick? I do not want a hallucination or self-induced hypnotic vision and think I'm seeing God!" Here is where the rubber meets the road. You will need to completely let go of your doubts and unbelief and trust in the Lord to experiment with opening your spiritual eyes. You will receive no witness until after the trial of your faith.[200] Then, you will ask yourself, "Whoa, was that really what I think it was?"

In an interesting 5th century apocryphal book called the Gospel of Mary, it reads:

> 5) Peter said to Mary, Sister we know that the Savior loved you more than the rest of woman.
> 6) Tell us the words of the Savior which you remember which you know, but we do not, nor have we heard them.
> 7) Mary answered and said, What is hidden from you I will proclaim to you.
> 8) And she began to speak to them these words: **I, she said, I saw the Lord in a vision and I said to Him, Lord I saw you today in a vision. He answered and said to me,**
> **9) Blessed are you that you did not waver at the sight of Me. For where the mind is there is the treasure.**
> **10) I said to Him, Lord, how does he who sees the vision see it, through the soul or through the spirit?**
> **11) The Savior answered and said, <u>He does not see through the soul nor through the spirit, but the mind that is between the two that is what sees the vision</u>** and it is [...]
> *(pages 11 - 14 are missing from the manuscript)*

---

[200] Ether 12:6

The ability to imagine eternal life and becoming one with God is crucial to having visionary experiences. Some develop this ability through *lectio divina,*[201] a slow, meditative study of the scriptures. True imaginations are called an "eye of faith," or "single eye," or the "mind's eye." Most scriptural references speak of imagination associated with evil, probably because that is the tendency of a corruptible man. But if it's good to exercise the imagination in a faithful way, wouldn't there be scripture to support that idea? Yes! See the following:

> **Do ye exercise faith** in the redemption of him who created you**? Do you look forward with an eye of faith, and view** this mortal body raised in immortality, and this corruption raised in incorruption, to stand before God to be judged according to the deeds which have been done in the mortal body? I say unto you, **can you imagine to yourselves that ye hear the voice of the Lord**, saying unto you, in that day: Come unto me ye blessed, for behold, your works have been the works of righteousness upon the face of the earth? Or **do ye imagine to yourselves that ye can lie** unto the Lord in that day, and say—Lord, our

[201] In Christianity, Lectio Divina (Latin for "Divine Reading") is a traditional Benedictine practice of scriptural reading, meditation, and prayer intended to promote communion with God and to increase the knowledge of God's Word. It does not treat Scripture as texts to be studied, but as the Living Word.

> works have been righteous works upon the face of the earth—and that he will save you? Or otherwise, **<u>can ye imagine</u> yourselves brought before the tribunal of God with your souls filled with guilt** and remorse, having a remembrance of all your guilt, yea, a perfect remembrance of all your wickedness, yea, a remembrance that ye have set at defiance the commandments of God? (Alma 5:15-18)

And then Alma writes more about this:

> And now, behold, **because ye have tried the experiment**, and planted the seed, and it swelleth and sprouteth, and beginneth to grow, ye must needs know that the seed is good. And thus, if ye will not nourish the word, **looking forward with an <u>eye of faith</u>** to the fruit thereof, ye can never pluck of the fruit of the tree of life. But if ye will nourish the word, yea, nourish the tree as it beginneth to grow, by your faith with great diligence, and with patience, **<u>looking</u> forward to the fruit** thereof, it shall take root; and behold it shall be a tree springing up unto everlasting life. (Alma 32:33, 40-41)

Moroni adds his witness:

> And neither at any time hath any wrought miracles until **after their faith; wherefore they first believed** in the Son of God. And there were many

> whose faith was so exceedingly strong, even before Christ came, who could not be kept from within the veil, but truly **saw with their eyes the things which they had beheld with an <u>eye of faith</u>**, and they were glad. (Ether 12:18-19)

I have done this very thing and can tell you unequivocally that it is a real experience, as real as if I had seen with my own *two eyes*.

How are you feeling? Are you ready to look and see the Lord? You can do this, I know it.

I AM READY

I have shared with you all my thoughts and experiences that have led up to the day that changed everything for me. You will probably have your own unique, custom-tailored experience, and the Lord will guide you in your preparations, but there are universal patterns that may be helpful. Most importantly, follow the Spirit.

Here is a short outline of what I did 24 hours leading up to my Second Comforter:

1. Began a fast about 24 hours before.
2. Set a time for the following morning to approach the Lord.
3. Visited some families in need and offered service and blessings.

4. Attended Church and thought deeply about things of the Spirit.
5. Woke up and made preparations for prayer without using the phone, computer, or other distractions. (I had a one-track-mind.)
6. Partook of the Sacrament by myself.
7. Asked for forgiveness.
8. Began offering praises of gratitude, and declarations of God's greatness.
9. Envisioned myself bathing in light and glory as I praised.
10. Began speaking in tongues as I used my personal prayer language of praise and love.
11. Asked the Lord if He would share His love and light with me. "Lord, may I come unto thee? What would thou have me to do?"
12. Allowed the vision to take shape.
13. Kept asking for more and allow the Spirit to guide.
14. I was not in a hurry; I was patient; I allowed my mind to search and see spiritually. I focused on details: what I saw, felt, and smelled.

"Verily, thus saith the Lord: It shall come to pass that every soul who forsaketh his sins and cometh unto me, and calleth on my name, and obeyeth my voice, and keepeth my commandments, shall see my face and know that I am;" (D&C 93:1)

The Visit

Chapter Fourteen

The following journal entry is exactly as it was written shortly after I had the experience. I tried to write as many details as I could remember. Some of the footnotes were added later to clarify my experiences. My hope is that you will ask yourself the question, "Can I do this? Should I try to do this? Do I want to do this?" I hope your answer is, "Yes!"

JANUARY 18, 2016 "MY SECOND COMFORTER"

Today I was resolved to spend some time taking the Sacrament and coming to the Lord in prayer. I desired to sanctify myself and to see my Lord and to be taught of Him. The experience I received was far more detailed than any I have had previously.

After I partook of the Sacrament, which I did beside my bed, sitting on the floor, I began by asking for forgiveness. I wanted to be clean before the Lord. Then I began to praise my God with gratitude and thankfulness. I prayed in tongues for about ten minutes. I would hear His voice in my head giving me encouragement and acknowledging my praise and worship. I kept saying and expressing my love for Him and my desire to be close to Him.

I asked that I might be taught and learn more and to be made holy.

I was told to imagine light coming upon me. I focused for a while, imagining great light, brighter than the sun, filling my entire being. From head to toe, I was bathing in the light. I even saw my cells at the atomic level. I tried to see the DNA filling with light. It was as if my entire spirit and body was being bathed. I was told to do this regularly, as I partook of the Sacrament, ate, drank, showered—as often as possible.

I was then told to relax and open my mind to a vision. I first saw myself standing on a ledge of a great mountain. My head was turned up as the wind and the light of day blew around me. I then saw the place where the brothers had gone earlier this year and built an altar. I looked around. It was in the summer; I was by myself feeling the awe for what we had done there. I knew that the area was now covered with snow, so I was seeing a vision of the place.

I then was above the earth. I was just above the atmosphere looking down at the blue earth, covered in small patches of clouds. I turned around and seemed to be in a room of glass where the walls and floor were transparent. It was very solid, yet I could see through it. For a moment I had the strange thought of whether there was dust on the floor, and in an instant I could see very closely that there was not as much as a speck.

There was a man in white with a rounded, close-cut beard standing behind the desk in front of me. His beard was white, his face was not thin, but full and healthy. His clothing was white and angelic without any special embroidery or extravagance.

Everything I was seeing in my mind seemed somewhat clouded, as if I had dust in my eyes and I was struggling to open them. I would see clearly and then it would go out of focus.

I asked him who he was and he said his name was Meleck. I don't know if I'm spelling it right. The first "e" was like the word "Eve." He began to smile at me. I never saw his mouth move when he spoke to me. I expressed my desire to him to know the Lord and to prepare myself. I asked where I was and was given knowledge that I stood above the United States. I asked more specifically who he was and was told that he was a messenger and that we had been friends for a long time and had known each other before.

I then saw what seemed like a crescent moon. It was a waning moon right before New Moon. Then in my mind I saw a blood moon. I wondered what it meant.

I suddenly began to see images in my mind. I saw a nuclear explosion, followed by more of them. I could see the large plume, followed by the great devastation below, as if I was standing upon the ground as the blast washed over the buildings.[202] I was shown that the nuclear attack was

---

[202] I remember brown and black dust blowing over me as I looked up at a building being wiped out.

limited, but that the country broke down and there was great rioting and war. I saw what looked like Muslim men yelling in the streets.[203] I think it was on the other side of the world.

I saw a large fire ball from space, the size of a small mountain, hit the Northern hemisphere and caused huge devastation upon the world.[204] Earthquakes, tidal waves, and smoke.

I was afraid and asked, "What am I supposed to do?" I was told to be at peace. I was then carried through a portal of light going upward very fast. I then came to a place of great brilliance and light and had the impression I was looking upon God's Throne. I felt unworthy and small and was given some kind of garment of light that gave me comfort.[205] I saw hosts of angels and beings of light, and others were darting across and above them. There was singing, but it was different than what I would expect. It was more like harmonic tones that seemed to be filled with praise. There was more to their singing than I understood. It was beautiful and glorious and I would have asked more questions, but my attention was upon the throne. There was a spinning galaxy of sorts, or stars, above the throne, which seemed to have multiple levels above and below. My

---

[203] There seemed to be hundreds and it was at night.
[204] At first it was dark, then it began to catch fire, and I knew it had entered our atmosphere.
[205] I did not put it on like regular clothing. It was as if it was thrown onto me.

eyes struggled to look upon it. I had the impression that the Adversary was allowed to come and witness against people at this court, which seemed odd to me. I will need to pray more about this.

I then began to praise God and felt great joy as I considered His holiness. I desired to be close to Him. I asked if I could come to Him in His garden. I don't know what made me consider asking this, but no sooner had I made this request than I was descending upon a beautiful landscape.

I was in the most beautiful place. Tall trees, a path of stone, and the garden had more color and richness than I had ever experienced. Gold seemed to be the prominent color. All the colors shimmered and seemed to be alive. There was a deep river of crystal clear water near the path. I walked a few steps then found myself floating. I entered the water and felt its form and resistance, and yet it was no trouble to move. As I submerged myself effortlessly, I saw large colorful fish swimming around and in front of me. I came out of the water and I noticed I was not wet. I then saw Jesus in the garden and I went to Him.

He was beautiful in His appearance. His hair was reddish brown; His face appeared smooth. His eyes were full of color and brilliance. I hugged Him and kissed His hands. It all felt so natural and effortless. Complete love and beauty. I saw the markings upon his hands. They were light and had a small "T" shape in them. I kissed His feet and felt the scar in His side. The entire experience was gentle and with love as a father would embrace a little child. Everything seemed to happen so quick, and yet it was completely unpretentious and comfortable. I don't remember everything that was spoken.[206]

I expressed gratitude for my wife and children. I was told that my wife was very special. I asked the Lord if we could have our Second Comforter experience with Him together and was told that we could. It doesn't happen often, but is according to our faith.

I was told to continue the process of filling my being with light and holiness—by fasting, prayer, and asking in faith—and that I would be ready for what must come. I expressed my concern that I was weak. My spirit is willing, but my flesh is a deterrent. He said I would be strengthened.

I saw a vision of a desolate place on earth. A young girl, broken and sick, about 11 years old. I held her, blessed her, and brought her to safety. I saw myself preaching repentance, baptizing, giving the Holy Ghost by the laying on of hands, and bringing them to safety, either by guiding them or taking them directly to Zion.

I was told to come back often.
Although all of this was in vision, as I sat on the floor of my bedroom, it was very alive in my mind. At times it was very clear and at times it was out of focus, and yet I knew that I

---

[206] I could feel everything and it was very tangible. He blessed me and told me of my mission.

was still there.[207] Now that I have had a taste I want more.[208] [209]

---

[207] D&C 76:12 "By the power of the Spirit our eyes were opened and our understandings were enlightened, so as to see and understand the things of God—"

[208] I had a mix of emotions as it ended. I was filled with love, shock, gratitude, and bewilderment. I had been praying for about an hour and a half.

[209] "Lord, what does it mean to have your Second Comforter? I felt that I had a pretty good idea, having read Joseph Smith's revelations, but perhaps there was more to it.

"He said that when you touch Him and meet Him it is a Second Comforter by definition. Often this occurs under great duress, but this was not the case with me, as I was simply doing what was required to part the veil. He said that there was still much to learn. I asked when I would be given the sealing power and the ability to bestow the Gift of the Holy Ghost. I was told that He would need to lay His hands upon me and by ordinance give me this power, but that it would not occur until it was time to gather Israel as was foretold. I would have time to prepare in faith. He told me not to worry, and that all things will happen at their proper time." (Visit dated January 22, 2016)

- NOTE FROM THE AUTHOR -

I always assumed that once I had my Second Comforter experience that I would not see the Lord again for a while. If it had not been for the invitation to "come often" I would not have attempted again so quickly. Since my first experience I have come back to him many times. Also, I am amazed at how willing the Lord is to answer my questions. I have asked every conceivable question since my first visit and I keep an ever changing list to ask for every time I go back. The only thing I was ever denied was a visit with Heavenly Grandfather, but was promised that would come at some point in the future. I have been introduced to the Father, Mother, and many others. God is so merciful and beyond comprehension in many ways! Everything has exceeded my expectations and the Lord does not hold back. I hope that by my sharing this experience and the journey that brought me to this point, that you will have the hope and desire to lay hold on the same thing and also obtain this unfathomable gift we call the Second Comforter.

Appendix I

January 26, 2016 "Vision of the Atonement"

This is a portion of a separate vision in which the Lord showed me the details of Gethsemane until the Resurrection. I have also included portions of subsequent visions that helped me to better understand these events. The Lord gave me permission to share this sacred information that you might understand two things: First, His atonement was vividly real, and second, all you need to do is ask, and you can see for yourself.

I then asked the Lord if I could witness the Gethsemane part of His atonement and within moments I was there. It was night and He was hunched over in the grass between the trees. He was in a white tunic and I watched for a short while; It was very vivid. I then asked, "Lord, will you teach me what I should know about all of this?" Here is where the vision began to unfold far more than I had expected.

I saw Jesus with Peter, James, John, and His wife, Mary, walking down a dirt path at night toward the garden. They went up a hill for a ways and came to a gate. They entered on the right and there was a building of stone. There was a small clearing and beyond it, a large orchard of olive trees. Jesus went directly to his normal place to pray after giving instructions to his apostles to watch and beware of the Adversary. The air was thick with bad spirits, very bad ones.

Jesus started to feel great despair, as did Mary who escorted him to his place. They spoke briefly, and she went away about 15 feet or so up the hill. This occurred on the southern part of the Mount of Olives. Jesus began to feel overwhelmed, within a short period, as the atonement was poured upon him. He felt the sin and pain of numerous souls flood over his spirit.[210] He lay on the ground and rolled in pain. At one point he called out to Mary to see if she was all right. She had experienced the same thing. Mary did not have to experience the rest, but was commanded to not come to Him until it was finished.[211]

He asked His Father if the cup was enough, for it felt like drinking bitterness in overwhelming amounts.

He checked on Mary and His apostles. The Adversary was filling the Garden with bad spirits and his presence was powerful.

Jesus returned to his place. The next phase literally knocked Him to the ground from a kneeling position. Each of these phases took well over an hour or more. Here he felt the pain of those who were recipients of the savagery of others: rape, murder, abuse, and all forms of pain. He felt their spiritual and emotional suffering, and He moaned in great

---

[210] I remember seeing a glimpse of numberless faces passing before my mind as if I was seeing what He was seeing for a brief moment.

agony. His body wretched on the ground while He sweat profusely.

Yeshuah called out to His Father, who came and held His hand and offered encouragement. At that moment there was a link of hands as each Father grasped hands in a chain of those who had paid the price of the atonement. I did not see how far this went. Mary was grieving terribly and Mother took her hand at the same time and there was a chain there too. After a short pause the Father left Him. Jesus checked on Mary and the Apostles and returned to His place.

The last phase came as Yeshuah was overcome with the pain of the perpetrators of these horrible acts. This is where he bled from every pore. His flesh agonized and he squirmed on the ground. His white tunic was mostly soaked with blood and sweat.

This was like swallowing such bitterness that it was overwhelming. He felt that His body would burst. He had never felt pain so severe. All the while Satan was mocking Him and tempting Him. This was when Jesus called out, “Father, why hast thou forsaken me?” His body bled everywhere. His daughter who had died as a small child and other close departed family came and comforted Him.

He said that before Gethsemane, Father had told Him that the way He would overcome would be to feel love, give love, and then forgive each person. By this He would overcome.[212]

His hair was dirty and grassy and He cried out many times. Mary was crying hard. When the last person was saved He immediately collapsed and felt relief. He had done what was required here.

When it was over it was still before dawn. Mary came to Him and they held each other and cried. She had brought clean clothes and ointment and a towel, which she used to take care of Him. They prayed and prepared.

He saw some lights of fire in the direction of the Apostles. The Temple guards were talking with them when Jesus approached. I saw a skirmish and Jesus was shackled and taken away up the dirt road again. This entire vision seemed to come in pieces. I feel I need to go back and search more to learn. He said that He would often ask to study what Father had done that He might learn.[213]

> After Mary and Him cleaned up and prayed He walked toward the Apostles. He awoke them just as the group of people from the Temple guard were coming. Jesus told Mary to go and He came back as the Apostles were speaking to the group.

---

[212] This detail was received as an answer to a question upon visiting with Him on March 17, 2016.

[213] It felt like an invitation or even a commandment to do this.

> It was still night, the guards were asking where Jesus was and the Apostles were acting like they didn't know. Jesus walked right up to the main guard, almost to his face and said He was the man. The main guard and three of the men recoiled and stumbled backward. They were frightened by Jesus stature as He was a large man too.
>
> Judas came up to Jesus and kissed him and called him Master. The guards aggressively grabbed Jesus and Peter struck the guard cutting off his ear. I saw Jesus rebuke Peter and heal the guard. The other guards attempted to grab the Apostles and they got away, but John's clothes were ripped off him except his undergarment. They beat Jesus down and shackled him. Many of the people spoke blasphemous things to Jesus as they dragged Him along the road toward the city. They had torches and lanterns and weapons, just like a mob. (Journal entry dated March 17, 2016)

I saw them throw him into a pit, which was about 10 feet deep and narrow. It had foul things at the bottom and Jesus landed on all fours and some of it hit His face. It was dark and He thought for a moment, "So, this is what death tastes like?" [214]

---

[214] I have not included all the detail from these visions. There was much regarding Caiaphas, Pilate, Herod, and other people. Unless I am instructed to publish that material I will keep it to myself.

I saw Him with Pilate. I saw Pilate's face. I saw Herod's face. I saw Him flogged. I saw him mocked by the Roman guards. I saw him before Pilate again with Barabbas. Barabbas had black hair and a cruel smile. They stood below Pilate with a Roman guard to the side of each of them. Jesus had the crown on his head, which was a mangled high cluster of the twisted thorny branch. The lacerations on his front and back were deep. Everything was like short clips of a movie.

> He showed Jesus to the crowd, which was mostly all Pharisees, and decided it best to scourge Jesus and release Him.[215] Jesus was taken to a place where they did such things connected to the fortress, an open area with a wood post. His hands were shackled and his clothes removed. The guards had Jesus' clothes put away, because they planned to keep them. There was one guard assigned to do the lashing. Many of the Roman soldiers watched, as if it were entertainment. The lashing man bragged about what he would do and tried to frighten Jesus by telling stories and making loud whip noises. The guards laughed and Jesus was silent. In His mind He was praying for the man and the guards.
>
> The man whipped Jesus with the lashing tool on his front and back. It was horrible. There were deep

[215] I was shown in a separate vision that four of Jesus' close disciples were among those in the crowd that condemned Him.

lacerations in some places. There were more on the back than the front. Jesus bled profusely and His entire body was red with blood. During the lashing as the guard would yell at him and the other soldiers laughed, Jesus would shout out, “Forgive them Lord, for they know not what they do!” Jesus demeanor stunned most of these men and by the end they were bewildered by Jesus’s reaction to the torture. He was carried by two guards into the main hall. They had some cloth under his arms and didn’t want to get Jesus’ blood on them.

In the hall He was sat in a chair and a purple scarf was placed over His shoulder, they put a reed with the flowery end in His hand and a crown of thorns was made. This was done by wrapping the thorny branch around the pole of which He had been whipped. It was a tall crown and when they pushed it on His head and it penetrated to the skull in some places. The guards treated Jesus as the King of the Jews, for they hated all things Jewish and enjoyed the mockery. Jesus took it all calmly and continued to forgive and love.

I saw Him before Pilate again and the crowd. He was wearing only his undergarment with the crown. They were a crazy mob. I saw Barabbas. I had seen him before in the first vision and he was the same. It was ironic that Barabbas was released, when his hatred for Rome was regularly expressed.

> I asked the Lord to only show me what I needed to see, some I had seen in previous visits. I saw Him carrying his cross, but now the undergarment was gone and he had only a loin cloth of sorts. Many women were wailing and following, which I don't understand who they were. Jesus spoke to them not to wail for Him but for themselves, which caused some to give Him a funny look. (Journal entry dated March 17, 2016)

I saw a long piece of light colored, yellowish wood, about five or six feet in length given to Him to carry. I think it may have weighed about 50 pounds. It was not as big as I thought and not a cross. He painfully put it over his shoulder, but had to drag it mostly. People spit and even some threw rocks at Him as he carried it through the street, past the temple, towards the same hill where he had suffered on the Mount of Olives. I sensed that he got the help from Simon the Cyrene, but I didn't see that part.[216]

> I saw Yeshua carrying his cross with great difficultly, as the guards whipped Him and yelled, because he was moving too slow. An older man with a grey beard shouted to the guards something like, "Can't you see he can't do it?" They suggested he carry the wood, which he did willingly, because he felt compassion. He swung the wood up on his shoulder effortlessly and held out his arm for

---

[216] I'm still amazed at how vivid the vision was, as if I was among the bystanders witnessing everything.

Yeshua to steady himself, and they walked up the hill together. Yeshua had a wound of some kind on his foot which made it all the more difficult to walk (a bruise from when he was thrown into the pit). He wore the tall crown of thorns upon his head, which was pitiful to look upon; it was a painful joke.

When he got to the spot toward the upper part of the Mount of Olives. He was thrown on the ground and I saw the guards hammer the nails through his hands and lower arms near the wrists. He exhaled sharply, but did not cry out in pain. He said that although the pain was agonizing He felt joy in His heart knowing He was fulfilling all righteousness and that it was not any worse than he had already suffered. I saw his mother, wife, and John from His perspective looking down from the cross. They were very emotional and John hugged Mary, His wife as she cried bitterly. Yeshua's eyesight was dim, but he could see them spiritually. He was thirsty and it effected His speech, but was able to say what He needed. The sky was dark, like a storm was approaching and the air was static, but no rain. When he died, there was a tremor, but it hit hardest in the area of the temple, where the veil broke. (This excerpt was from a later vision dated February 1, 2016.)

Above the Garden, which He passed, were some Olive trees, large and broken. For some reason, I didn't get to see the nails driven through his hands, but I knew that the guards were not accustomed to seeing such a large man as Jesus and they were worried; they drove an extra set of nails through His lower arms near the wrist. They then tied ropes to the wood beam and dragged Jesus up the tree where it was tied and secured. Then a single nail was driven through His feet. His body was covered in blood and much of the blood had turned black. He wore a loin cloth of sorts. I know there were two others crucified near Him, but I didn't pay much attention.

I saw a large sign above him in the tree. It was really big, much bigger than I expected. The guards had made three signs and each was carried to and positioned above those crucified. It was perhaps 2X3 feet in size.

Mary the Mother, Mary Magdalene, and John had followed the procession and witnessed much from a distance. People spat upon Him and some threw stones, which inflicted more damage to his flesh. Mostly people came and watched who were curious. You could see the temple from the hill where he hung. Jesus did not face the direction of the temple.

> I next saw Yeshuah hanging on the cross. The thieves were in the trees next to Him and could not be seen by Jesus but heard. Jesus said to me that he would not take the vinegar because it was like a drug and He wanted to be fully aware. It was not proper. I'm not sure what He meant by that. When He said, "Father where art thou?" it was because he could not hear the Father's voice. Then, Father said to Jesus, "It is finished!" and Jesus repeated

> this out loud, “It is FINISHED!” He came forth in the spirit from his body and the Heavens opened. Jesus said it was the most music and praise He had ever seen. He was embraced by the Father and all those who were close to Him. It was so much joy, an infinite celebration! I saw glimpses of the event and it was like nothing I can explain. (Journal entry dated March 17, 2016)

I did not see all the other details. The next I knew, He was dead and was being taken down from the cross. His body was wrapped and laid in the tomb. The images in my mind were passing quickly. I saw Him looking down at His body as it lay in the dark tomb. When He healed his body, His spirit entered it again, and He was resurrected. Yeshuah then walked straight through the stone wall and the joy He felt was unmeasurable. He first went to the site of the crucifixion and stood before the spot where he had been a few days before. It was a time of reflection.

> I asked if he went straight to the cross, as I saw yesterday and was told, “No.” I saw Him walk through the stone and stand outside the tomb. It was still dark. The Roman guards were scared speechless. Then there was an earthquake and the angels rolled back the stone. The Lord felt compassion for the guards and blessed them. He then went and stood before the place of the crucifixion and contemplated, then he went to Gethsemane and contemplated some more. After this He went to the Temple below the Mount of

> Olives and contemplated some more. Shortly thereafter He appeared to Mary. It was early dawn when He saw her. (Later vision dated January 27, 2016)

I saw Mary, wearing black with something white in her hands, approach the tomb. I saw Yeshuah embrace her, and that was the end of the vision.

There was so much, and Jesus talked to me through the whole thing, like someone giving a play by play of their home video. I was told that I could take my time and learn more if I chose to come back to the vision. There is much more. The vision lasted about three hours, and I think I could have been there eight hours and not seen it all. I will go back as I think the Lord wants me to learn more and reflect upon this great act of His compassion. I am a little surprised by the emotion I felt as I witnessed all of this. My heart ached, I felt numb and horrified, and yet, because He was with me, I didn't cry. He was with me! I felt peace during it all. I felt gratitude and profound respect. I felt like I was being schooled in something very important and that I must dig deeper and study everything.

I thanked the Lord and hugged Him. I held His hands and kissed them. I could feel the strength of His body. He smiled and was pleased. I said, "Lord, I want to learn everything that will help me. Do I share these experiences with others?" He said, "Yes," and that I would know where to stop and not to share. Now are the days of the revealing of all things to those who will hear. He said I must learn as much as I can so that I will know how to bless others.[217]

[217] This last paragraph is the end of my visit experienced March 17, 2016.

Appendix 2

A PRAYER OF PRAISE

My personal prayer written after receiving the Second Comforter:

O thou Father, who art exalted in the Heavens, I will sing praises unto thy name.

Thou art full of compassion and gracious long suffering, full of mercy and truth. Thou art my Father, my God, my shield and my glory forever.

How excellent is thy name above all the earth, and thy glory above all the heavens. I will praise thee with my whole heart, for I recognize thy majesty and all thy marvelous works.

I will praise the name of the Most High; for thou judgest righteously upon thy throne.

Thou art my refuge from the storm in times of trouble. I shall put my trust in thee; thou art my rock and my deliverer and my strength. I have cried unto thee and thou hast healed me.

Lord, thou art in thy temple, in the holy throne of Heaven and thy words are pure and I have partaken of thy mercy. Are my hands clean and my heart pure? May I ascend unto thy holy tabernacle? Show me thy ways Lord, teach me thy paths. Thy commandments are pure and thy judgments are true, and have enlightened my eyes. Thou art holy; our fathers trusted in thee and so shall I.

Lord, who shall abide in thy tabernacle? Only he that speaketh truth in his heart, and walketh uprightly. May the words of my mouth and the thoughts of my heart be acceptable in thy sight.

Thou looketh down from Heaven with thy all seeing eye to find if there are any who seek thy face. I will behold thy face in righteousness, and I will be satisfied when I awake in thy presence. I shall always seek thee. My soul has thirsted to be in thy presence and my heart has hungered for thy blessing. God, be not far from me; comfort me and bring me to thy bosom. Guide me with thy council, receive me in thy glory.

Wilt thou hear me from the highest heaven with the saving strength of thy right hand?

Some will trust in armies, in weapons, or in themselves, but I shall trust in thee; because thou hast given me the shield of thy salvation and has held me up with thy right hand and thy gentleness has lifted me up. Thou hast girded me with thy strength in battle and subdued those who desired to destroy me. My strength is in thee Lord, not the arm of flesh.

Thou hast made my steps sure beneath my feet and led me through rough passages. Thou art the good shepherd that watches over me, that provides, nourishes, and protects. Thou created the heavens and knowest each of thy creations by name, and we are thy sons and are worthy of thy attention. I praise thy name, O Lord!

Thy tender mercies and loving kindness are always before me. Teach me thy way Lord, lead me on a plain path. Do not let the foot of pride and the hand of Satan remove me from thy favor. Help me, O God of my salvation, and deliver me from evil.

Wilt thou light my candle that I might be a light for others, that I might teach by the power of thy Spirit and bring home thy children?

O redeem Israel, my Lord, from her troubles, and the House of Jacob, that we may gather them in to safety. Thou art the Lord of Hosts and the God of Jacob. Wilt thou send the rod of thy strength out of Zion; for thou art the God that doest great wonders. Great is the Lord and mighty is the King that shall dwell in Zion with the saints!

Thou art clothed with honor and majesty and thy work is glorious and thy righteousness and mercy endureth forever.

Thou hast:

- Created the earth that we may have joy and learning and triumph over evil.

- Brought forth the Book of Mormon and holy scripture, through thy prophets to enlighten and guide us.
- Given me hope and faith and understanding of all things spiritual.
- Shown me the way by knowing of thy life and teachings.
- Given me, by the faith of our fathers, a free land.
- And above all, thou hast redeemed me from the pains of sin that I may return to thy presence.

Lord, teach me to do thy will. Cause me to know thy ways and how I should walk. Quicken me, O Lord, according to thy loving kindness and bring my soul out of trouble.

I shall praise thy holy name forever, even Yeshua Messiah, my everlasting God!

Amen

Email Address:

It would bring me great joy to learn of your story when you have your Second Comforter experience. Please contact me at:

mysecondcomforter@gmail.com